MICHELANGELO

&

the Creation of the Sistine Chapel

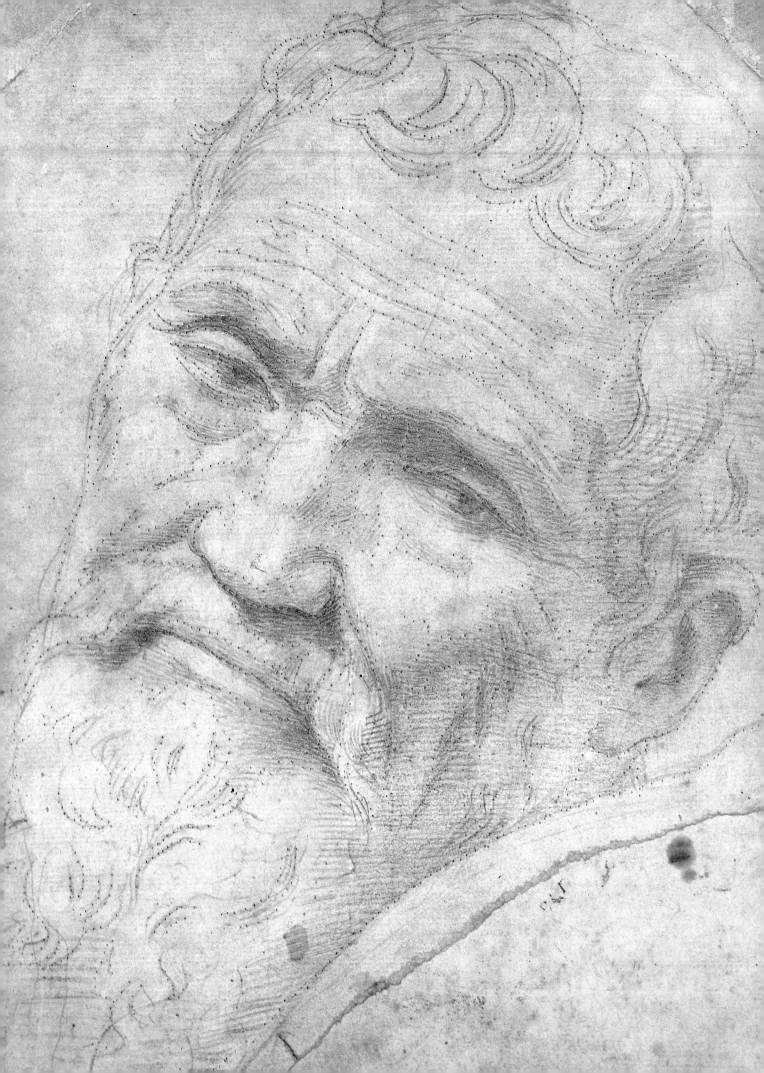

MICHELANGELO
& the Creation of the Sistine Chapel

ROBIN RICHMOND

CRESCENT BOOKS
NEW YORK • AVENEL

Photographic Acknowledgements

All photographs of the restored ceiling are by courtesy of Nippon Television. The sources of additional photographs are as follows:

Biblioteca Medicea Laurenziana, Florence 121, 124; The Bridgeman Art Library 45, 47 bottom right, 134 right; Reproduced by courtesy of the British Museum 25; Robert Harding Picture Library 40; Index/Bencini 27 left; Index/Orsi Battaglini 38/39; Metropolitan Museum, New York 26; Gift of Quincy Adams Shaw Jr and Mrs Marion Shaw Houghton, Courtesy, Museum of Fine Arts Boston 30 right; Scala Istituto Fotografico Editoriale S.p.A. 14, 16, 17, 18, 20, 21, 22, 28, 29 left, 30 left, 31, 32, 33, 34/35, 36, 38 left, 41, 42, 43, 44, 46, 47 left, 49, 50, 58, 59, 65 bottom, 120, 125, 126, 127; Staatliche Graphische Sammlung, Munich 27 right; Staatliche Museen zu Berlin 4 right; The Teylers Museum, Haarlem 2, 97 bottom; Windsor Castle, Royal Library © 1991 Her Majesty the Queen 37.

Frontispiece: Cartoon for a portrait of Michelangelo by Daniele da Volterra, about 1550.

First published in Great Britain in 1992 by Barrie & Jenkins Limited Reprinted in 1993

Text copyright © 1992 by Robin Richmond Photographs (of the Sistine Chapel ceiling) copyright © Nippon Television Network Corporation Produced and developed by Belitha Press Ltd, 31 Newington Green, London N16 9PU Designed by Gillian Riley Edited by Marilyn Malin

This 1995 edition published by Crescent Books, distributed by Random House Value Publishing, Inc. 40 Engelhard Avenue, Avenel, New Jersey 07001.

Random House New York • Toronto • London • Sydney • Auckland

Library of Congress Cataloging-in-Publication Data

Richmond, Robin
    Michelangelo and Sistine Chapel / Robin Richmond.
        p. cm.
    Includes bibliographical references and index.
    ISBN 0-517-14194-9
    1. Michelangelo Buonarroti, 1475–1564––Criticism and interpretation.
    2. Mural painting and decoration. Renaissance––Vatican City. 3. Mural painting and decoration. Italian––Vatican City. 4. Sistine Chapel (Vatican Palace, Vatican City) I. Title.
    ND823.B9R53 1995
    759.5--dc20   *95–14238*
                                                              CIP

10, 9, 8, 7, 6, 5, 4, 3, 2

Printed in Hong Kong for Imago

For

J.A.H.

Veggio nel tuo bel viso, signor mio,
quel che narrar mal puossi in questa vita . . .

Michelangelo *Rime*, c.1534

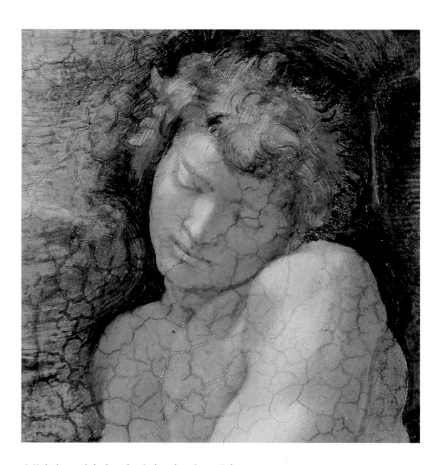

Michelangelo's head of the sleeping Adam,
from the panel depicting the Creation of Eve.

Contents

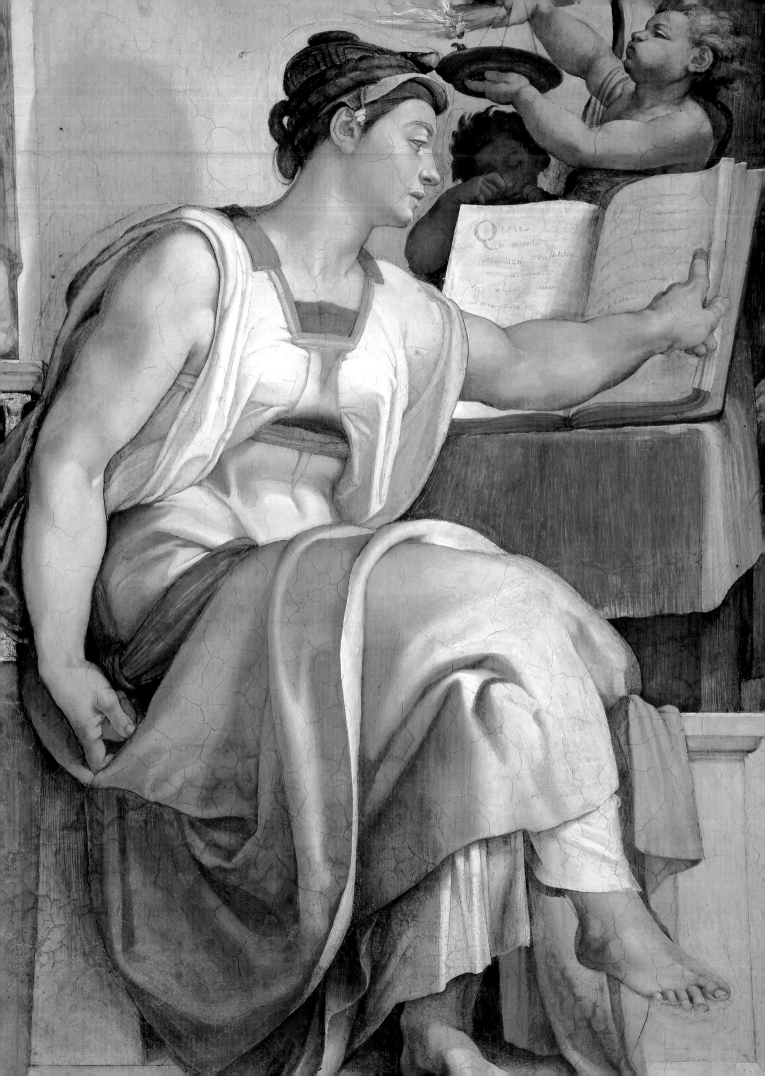

🙋 *Foreword*

Why should there be another book on Michelangelo? Another work on an artist who is the most exhaustively documented subject in the history of art needs some defence. Is there room on the crowded library bookshelves for any more? There are those who believe that an artist ultimately stands or falls on the strength of his or her work alone and, as an artist myself, I sympathise with this view. Reading about artists and the circumstances that nurture and mould their creativity can only partly help to unravel the mystery that is at the core of their art. Most artists themselves find it difficult to explain in words what it is they do and Michelangelo was no exception. But there are always new things that can be said about art and the greater the art, the more that can be said about it. The challenge is to make it easy to understand, without resorting to art history's private language which, like any discipline, is larded with jargon; and there are many brilliant books on Michelangelo that achieve this.

The reason for this book, however, is that over the last ten years something extraordinary has happened to change our ideas about Michelangelo. Through the generosity of the Nippon Television Network, the Vatican has been able to employ its own team of highly skilled restorers to clean, restore and conserve the ceiling painted by Michelangelo in the first years of the sixteenth century. This book has the privilege of using the photographs of this process and of the final result, courtesy of NTV Japan.

The restoration of Michelangelo's ceiling has caused bitter controversy among scholars, historians, conservators, restorers, scientists and artists. Why? The answer to this is complicated. Perhaps my own reactions may provide a way to understand the argument that followed the news, in 1980, that the Sistine Chapel was going to be cleaned.

I grew up in Rome and was so familiar with Michelangelo that I never questioned whether his work looked now as it had in his own day. I took it for granted that one could hardly make out the figures on Michelangelo's ceiling, so deeply were they hidden in dark shadow. Michelangelo's own evaluation of his talent for painting was accepted by many scholars and artists. 'I am no painter,' he wrote again and again. So the grey, melancholy scenes on the Sistine ceiling have been interpreted in the past as

The Erithraean Sibyl (see page 57) after cleaning.

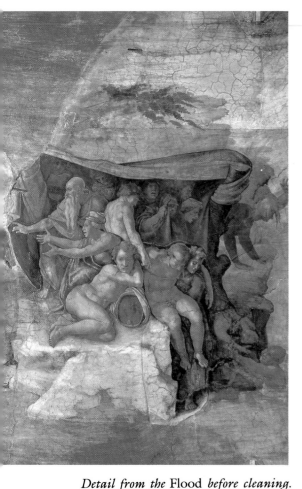

Detail from the Flood *before cleaning.*

Detail from one of the lunettes after cleaning, showing Michelangelo's shimmering use of colour.

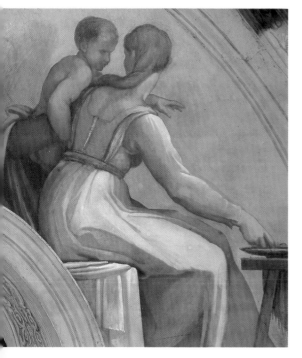

lacking what artists called 'painterliness', an elusive quality referring to an easy relationship with colour expressed with fluency. Such was the established wisdom in certain quarters about Michelangelo's skill as a painter. Even I knew from childhood that Michelangelo was a moody, difficult man who fought with the Pope. I had seen *The Agony and the Ecstasy*. Why shouldn't his ceiling be as black as his moods? It seemed obvious. The great Michelangelo scholars revered him as an artist preoccupied with form at the expense of colour. When it came to discussing the restoration in the late 1980s and the world press began to report disapproval among the *cognoscenti*, lesser mortals such as I had no right to comment. I certainly was in no position to make a judgement – although such was my love for Michelangelo's work that I had chosen to hold my eccentric, noisy wedding in the Campidoglio, one of Michelangelo's most stately creations.

When I heard about the restoration of the Sistine Chapel, I thought: 'Here they go again, using technology as the answer to everything. The whiter than white school of art history. Painting as laundry.' Like many artists, I felt that a great master's art must remain forever untouched by the 'evils' of science. It is a common prejudice of artists. There were many who considered that the restoration obliterated Michelangelo's final intentions and would remove his touch.

After many visits to the scaffolding in the Sistine Chapel, spent looking at and even touching the ceiling, I am convinced that this view was wrong. I have examined the facts and discussed the restoration extensively with the Vatican technicians and scientists over many years, and am persuaded that what I and other much greater scholars thought of as Michelangelo's gloomy, dark and melancholy painting style is the accumulation of almost five hundred years of soot, grime and misguided human interference.

As you can see from the brilliant and extremely accurate photographs in this book, we were all wrong about Michelangelo. His work emerges from the cleaning as a miracle of painting. Always his own worst enemy, Michelangelo has convinced critics down the centuries that he was only a reluctant, unsuccessful painter; but his use of colour, its delicate veils of shimmering lilacs, greens and yellows, is breathtaking. Where the ceiling was oppressive and heavy before, it now seems light enough to float away into the sky that is newly visible above the figures. Nothing has been taken away except our prejudices. Accusations that the ceiling has been industrially 'scrubbed' with a chemical akin to a household cleaner are hysterical and untrue. The Vatican team have developed their methods with care and rigour, as can be seen in Chapter 7, on the restoration. Their love, their *simpatia*, for Michelangelo is very obvious.

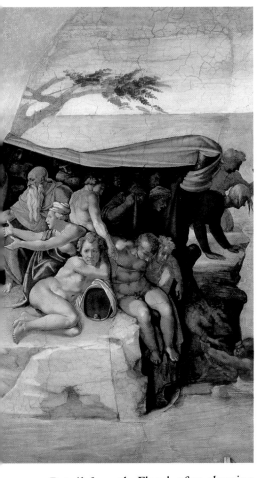

Detail from the Flood *after cleaning.*

Perhaps a mistake *was* made in the early days of the restoration, and it must be mentioned because it added fuel to the critics' fire. In 1986, photographs were published in the world press taken in harsh artificial light which is hostile to fresco painting. These pictures made the ceiling look garish, crude and almost psychedelic in colour. It was only when I visited the ceiling and saw it for myself that I realised how misleading photographs can be. The lighting has been carefully modulated now. Light no longer bounces off the walls and ceiling, but seems to glow from within the painting. It is less fierce, because it no longer needs to be. The painting, now clean, seems to have its own inner light.

Art and Science, the past and the present, the sable brush and the computer have all come together in this project in a way that would have delighted the Renaissance humanists of Michelangelo's circle. Michelangelo, a man not averse to speaking his own mind, however unpopular his views, would have been fascinated both by the process of the restoration and by the backbiting and sniping that has ensued.

This book is not a biography of Michelangelo, nor is it an exhaustive account of his life's work. What I have tried to do is to describe the events leading up to the creation of the Sistine Chapel ceiling and to communicate my own understanding of who Michelangelo was, as a man as well as an artist. I have made my own translations of some of his many letters and poems, and also of contemporary accounts of his life.

The best way to get under Michelangelo's skin and understand the atmosphere of his life and times is to read his own words and those of his friends. Fortunately much of his correspondence survives, and examples are interspersed throughout this book. There are almost five hundred letters by him in existence and hundreds of letters *to* him, making him one of the most documented artists in history.

The letters make delightful reading. His self-confident, sometimes petulant, often kindly voice jumps out of them across five centuries. His preoccupations are decidedly modern: the hassles of money problems and health worries and his demanding family.

We hear him lamenting the presence of an overly dependent and demanding parent. At one point, in 1511, in the final, difficult stages of the Sistine Chapel painting, you can almost hear the wail in his voice as he writes to his feckless father Lodovico, 'Don't you bother to read my letters?'

I have translated a selection of the letters, mostly the ones from Michelangelo to his father Lodovico and his nephew Lionardo. The subject of money is ever present. You will constantly notice the mention of the *spedalingo*. This refers to the bursar of the Church of Santa Maria Nuova, in Florence, where Michelangelo had an account. Unlike other banks of Florence at this time,

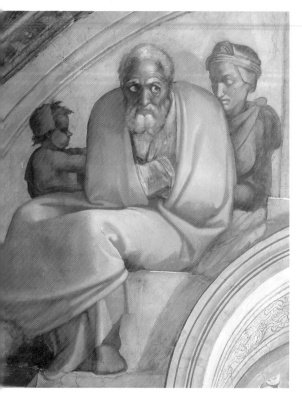

Detail from the lunette of Jacob and Joseph.

which were insecure institutions, this account yielded five per cent more interest on capital, and was more stable than a bank. The *spedalingo* also acted as a real estate agent from time to time, buying and selling land and properties. Michelangelo was involved in this activity as well.

Some scholars have commented that it is unfair to judge Michelangelo's relationship with his father on the basis of these letters. They give the impression that Lodovico persecuted Michelangelo with constant demands for money. There is no doubt that Michelangelo *felt* that it was necessary to support his relations, and perhaps they exploited his sense of family duty. He was a very responsible and responsive son, brother, uncle and friend. We should remember that Italians live in a family-centred culture. Michelangelo was no exception. Many people think of great artists as springing out of nowhere. But Michelangelo's family problems are as banal and irritating as those of us mere mortals.

Michelangelo was a central player on the stage of sixteenth-century Italian culture, and every star has his or her acolytes. Ascanio Condivi and Giorgio Vasari were admirers of Michelangelo and were keen to immortalise him in prose. Extracts from their work are on pages 146–149. Vasari's first monograph published in 1550 was not to Michelangelo's liking, but he wrote an even more flattering portrait of the artist in 1568, four years after his death. Vasari was an artist himself, who designed Michelangelo's tomb in Santa Croce, but he had a way of being 'economical with the truth'. We can assume that Condivi's 1553 account is more truthful, since Michelangelo himself helped Condivi with the details. It is certainly very immediate and has some of the 'authority of an autobiography', as Charles Holroyd wrote in 1903. The fact remains that the truth about Michelangelo cannot be found in any writings, whether his own or anyone else's, only in the work.

I am indebted to everyone who helped me with this book. First, to my parents, who gave me Rome and introduced me to art and to Michelangelo; to Joan and Robert Cook for their constant enthusiasm and hospitality; to the Vatican team, particularly Bruno Barratti and Maurizio Rossi, who endured endless questions with endless patience; to Maestro Gianluigi Colalucci and Dr Fabrizio Mancinelli of the Vatican Museums for their kindness and keen interest in my project; to Giuseppe Basile at the Istituto del Restauro; to Nicholas Wadley for his very helpful comments on the text; to Alison Richmond for consistently lively argument on conservation; to Belitha Press; to my much-more-than-editor Marilyn Malin for her unwavering belief in this book through all its vicissitudes; to Treld Bicknell for wisdom and encouragement; to Gillian Riley for months of Michelangelo talk and beautiful design; to Nippon Television and Hideo Aoki of Motovun, who made the whole thing possible but have in no way attempted to influence the views expressed, which are my own; and finally to my children, Adam and Saskia, who probably know more about Michelangelo than is necessary for a growing family, and to James for help with Control-F10.

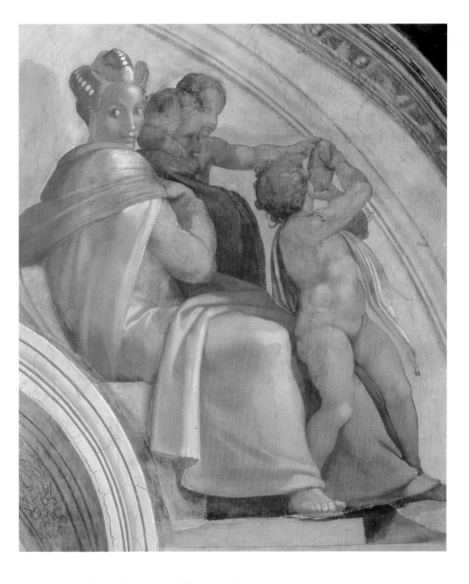

Family scene from the lunette of Jacob and Joseph.

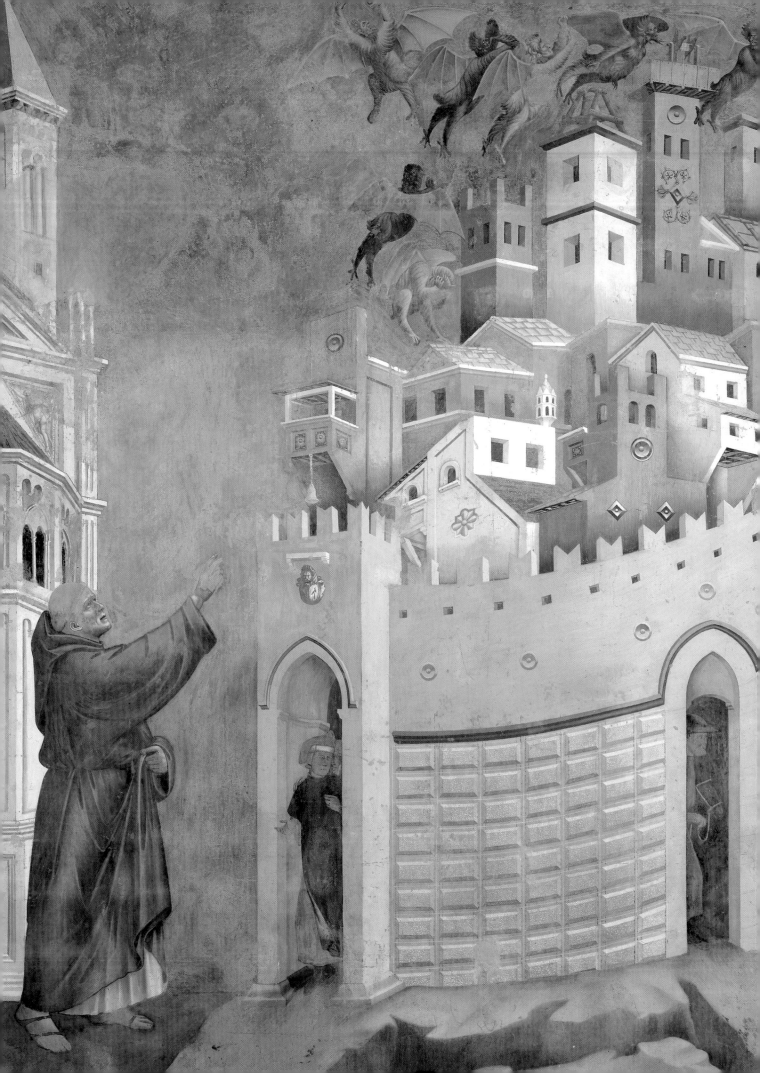

Introduction:
An Artist of the Renaissance

In one of Woody Allen's early films, he is dressed as a medieval man, exhorting his companion to hurry up, 'or before you know it the Renaissance will be here, and we'll all be painting'. It has always stayed in my mind, because the joke it makes about history is profound. How do we know that the period of history which we in the twentieth century refer to so casually as 'the Renaissance' was felt at the time to be distinct?

There is no doubt that changes took place in Europe from the end of the thirteenth century onwards, and in cultural and artistic terms they were based on a rediscovery of the ancient world. People at that time were not unaware of living in a period of great excitement and creative fervour in the arts, sciences and humanities. But what seems to us today to be a neat, self-enclosed episode in history is perhaps not an accurate picture. The edges are ragged. The period of the Renaissance has no clear beginning or end. It was a slow organic evolution in social values that expressed itself in art, politics, literature and science. This took place in Europe as a whole, but flowered particularly brilliantly in Italy.

The term *Renaissance* is owed mainly to the book by the famous nineteenth-century scholar, Jacob Burkhardt, *The Civilisation of the Renaissance in Italy*, but it was used enthusiastically in Michelangelo's lifetime by his friend and biographer Giorgio Vasari, in 1550. His word, *rinascita*, means 'rebirth' in English, which translates gracefully into the French 'renaissance'. The Oxford English Dictionary defines the Renaissance very fairly as 'the revival of arts and letters under the influence of classical models in the fourteenth to sixteenth centuries'.

The reasons for this evolution in social values are complex. They concern, among other things, advances in trade and world travel, manufacture of goods and commerce, discoveries in nature and analyses of natural phenomena, religion and changing systems of belief.

Renaissance Man was familiar with many disciplines and called himself a *humanist*. Sadly, women were not often considered important in such matters, with some rare exceptions such as Michelangelo's great friend and confidante, Vittoria Colonna, the

Giotto, 1267–1337: St Francis of Assisi expelling the Devils from Arezzo. *A medieval theme illustrated with an early use of perspective, and a naturalistic portrayal of the saint.*
(See also page 58 et seq.*)*

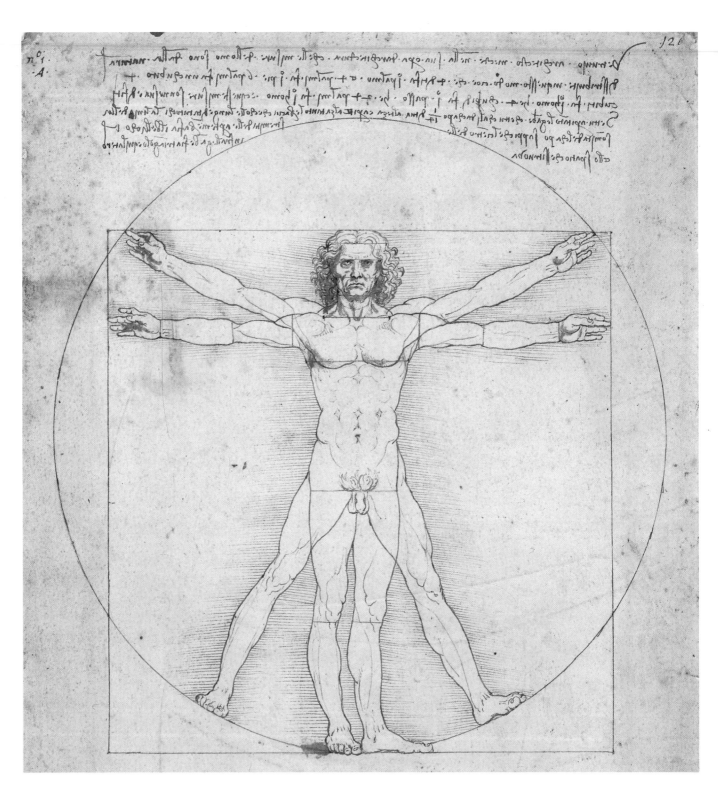

'Man is the measure of all things': Leonardo da Vinci drew this diagram to show how the proportions of the human body relate to the circle and the square.

Marchioness of Pescara. In *The Dignity of Man*, published in 1487, the great writer and philosopher Pico della Mirandola states categorically: 'Nothing is more admirable than Man.' This could be a slogan for the Renaissance.

The humanist belief that the disciplines of art and science, philosophy and politics, have blurred edges is fundamental to Renaissance thinking. Politicians, as we would now call them,

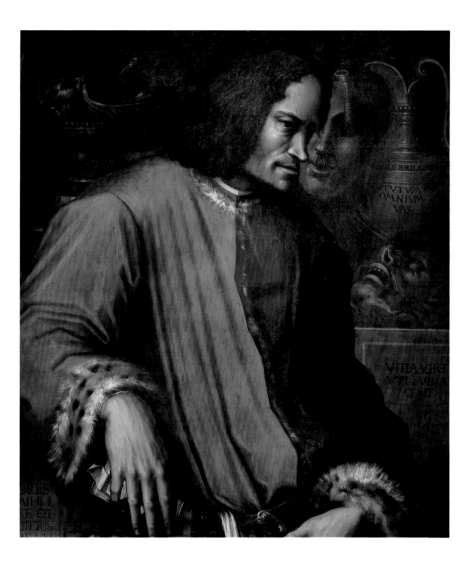

Portrait of Lorenzo de' Medici by Giorgio Vasari, about 1530.

were often intellectuals like Lorenzo de' Medici, Michelangelo's patron, and Niccolò Machiavelli, author of *The Prince*, a seminal work on the art of government. Artists might be scientists, like Leonardo da Vinci, and Popes might be military generals like Julius II. This fluidity of roles is very different from our society which forces people into pigeon holes. Humanism does not count for much in the twentieth century.

There are those who say that the Renaissance began with the printing of the three-volume Bible by Johannes Gutenberg of Mainz in 1456, and that it ended with the early death of Raphael of Urbino, painter and rival of Michelangelo, in 1520. Some people would maintain that its beginnings can be traced at least a century earlier to the period known as the Early Renaissance. But there is no doubt that Michelangelo Buonarroti, in the first part of his long career, expressed the ideals and technical mastery which we associate with the High Renaissance. There are many different strands to the story. Let us look at them briefly.

The emergence of a powerful and wealthy centralized Church provided a tremendous stimulus for the production of religious

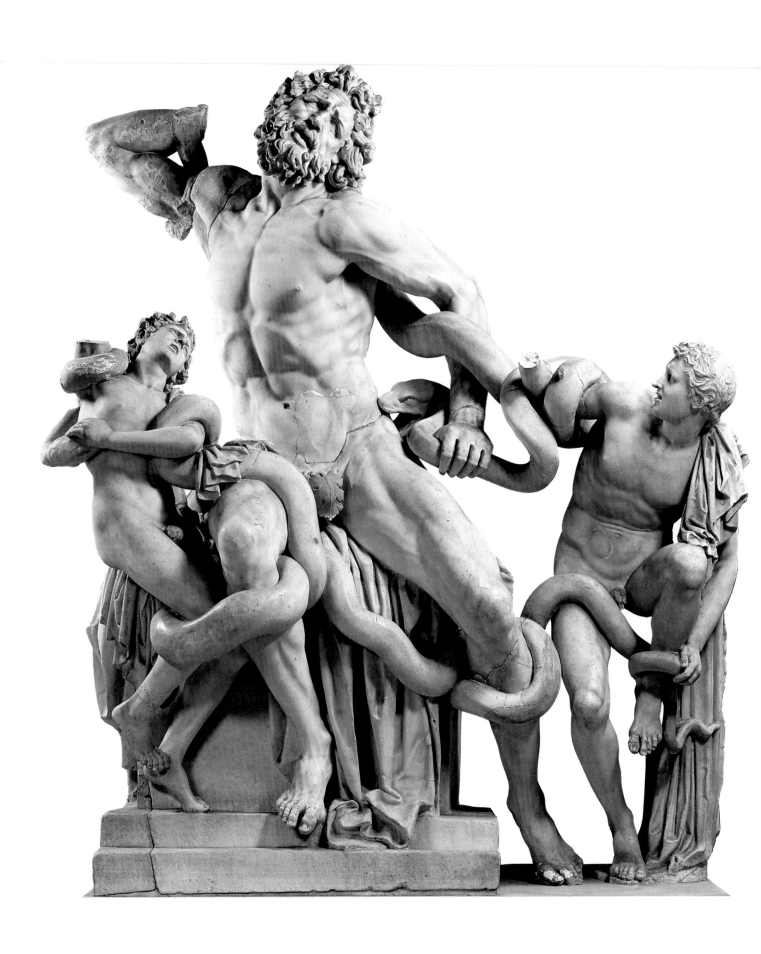

art, particularly in the Church's native land – Italy. This Church also had its critics, and a protesting voice was to be heard. In 1517, the monk Martin Luther of Saxony published his ninety-five 'theses', castigating the corrupt and money-centred attitudes of the Catholic Church. The effects of the schism that resulted, the Reformation, and the rise of Protestantism, are with us today.

Trade among different nations flourished during this time between Europe and the East. The great port of Venice traded with Constantinople and the Black Sea, Africa and Europe. Ships brought back luxury goods such as silk, furs, precious metals, cloth and spices. One effect of this was to open out the closed feudal society with its fixed and hierarchical social organization. Trade brought with it many changes in society. Travel and the exploration of the world exposed Europe to new civilizations and cultures, forcing a re-evaluation of life at home, particularly in Italy which was in the forefront of trade.

As early as the thirteenth century, in 1260, Marco Polo had left Europe for foreign lands, and men such as Christopher Columbus continued in this spirit of exploration. In the same year, 1492, that Columbus discovered the Americas, Florence, the centre of the Italian Renaissance, mourned the death of one of the great figures of the age, Lorenzo de' Medici, known as Lorenzo the 'Magnificent'. Michelangelo owed to this man the start of his illustrious career, for Lorenzo encouraged and supported the young artist.

Other events played a part as the Renaissance developed. Constantinople, the ancient capital of the Eastern Roman Empire and long-standing centre of Christian learning and also of classical knowledge, was invaded and sacked by the Turks in 1453 and as a result there was a significant migration of scholars to Central Europe. The works of ancient Greece and Rome had never been completely forgotten in the West, but in the Renaissance they were rediscovered, republished and studied afresh.

The first printing presses brought the works of classical philosophy, history and literature to a wider community of scholars. The strict control exercised by the Church over the study of science and nature was to be challenged by the first of the scientists of the modern age. Nicolaus Copernicus, the Polish astronomer, published *De Revolutionibus Orbium Coelestium* (Concerning the Revolution of the Planets) in 1453, turning ideas of the universe inside out. He proved, through observation of the heavens and through mathematics, that 'the centre of the earth is not the centre of the universe' because the earth, like other planets, revolves around the sun. This was in all senses shocking, because its inference was that Man was not at the

Laocoön, c.150 BC, Hellenistic – Roman period. Michelangelo was present at the excavation in Rome in 1506 of this famous marble statue by Agesandros, Polydorus and Athenodorus of Rhodes. The statue depicts the Trojan priest Laocoön and his sons crushed to death by snakes as a punishment for warning the Trojans about the wooden horse. This theme of divine retribution and physical torment had a profound influence on Michelangelo.

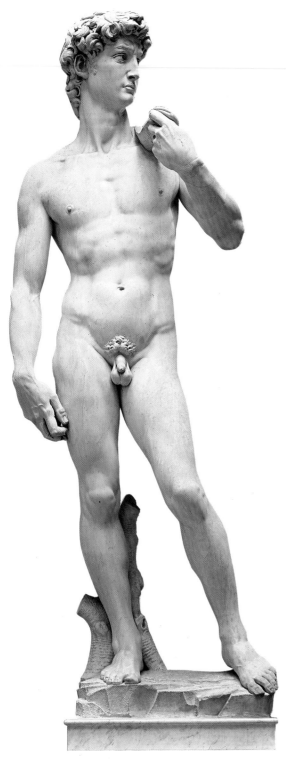

centre of everything. It was unacceptable to society and to the Church for at least a hundred years.

Michelangelo is one of the most important figures of this extraordinary period. His work expresses the desires and aspirations of his society in a pure, undiluted form. It incorporates the desire that was an essential part of the Renaissance to awaken the dormant, but not dead, forms of the ancient world. The beauty of classical Greek and Roman sculpture inspired him, in sculpture and in painting. The philosophy of the ancient Greeks, with their interest in concepts of Beauty and Truth, merges with a strong belief in Christianity and its tenets.

When we look at the works of Michelangelo, we are forced to think about our own ideas of 'what Art is about', and can see that they were determined more than five hundred years ago.

David *by Michelangelo, 1501–1504. The huge marble block, over fourteen feet high, had already been worked on by two other sculptors before the young Michelangelo was commissioned. He chose to portray the tense moment of resolution and apprehensiveness as the young David poised his sling for the triumphant blow that killed Goliath. The statue was positioned in front of the Palazzo Vecchio in Florence to celebrate the civic glories of the city. It was moved to its present site in the Accademia in 1873 and replaced by a full-sized copy.*

1 Michelangelo's Early Life, 1475-94

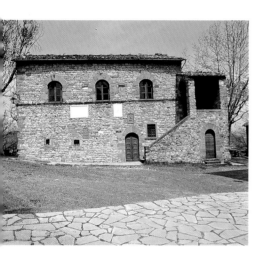

Michelangelo was born in this house in Caprese on 6 March 1475.

Michelangelo was born early in the morning of 6 March 1475, at Caprese, in the province of Tuscany. He was born to Lodovico di Leonardo di Buonarroti Simoni and Francesca di Neri di Miniato del Sera. At the time, Lodovico was *podestà* of this small community, which was a position of responsibility and authority similar to that of mayor or chief magistrate. This may seem like a stable family background for Michelangelo's early years, but the reality was very different and was to cast a long shadow over his life. The sadness of his early years can tell us a great deal about a man who, as an adult, felt alone and separate from the world he lived in.

Lodovico's appointment as *podestà* was almost over when his second son, Michelangelo, was born. The position was for a year and was one of the few jobs of responsibility that he ever held. He was a man who felt that work was beneath his dignity, preferring to rest upon the reputation of the Buonarroti-Simoni family which had been established in Florentine society for over three hundred years. By 1475, his family's fortunes had dwindled to very modest proportions. All Lodovico possessed was a share of a house in Florence and a smallholding at Settignano, not far from the city. He had little money, a growing family and a sick young wife.

Michelangelo was born into a family burdened by problems, and his birth made even more difficulties for his parents. His mother, Francesca, was still a teenager. She had been weakened by two births in as many years and was very frail. Michelangelo was dispatched to a stonecutter and his wife, who tended a farm at Settignano, to be looked after. As an infant he was nursed at the breast by the stonecutter's wife, and as an adult he would joke that he absorbed his love of stone through her milk.

Francesca produced three more sons for Lodovico. Lionardo was Michelangelo's older brother, born in 1473, and Michelangelo was followed by Buonarroto, born in 1477, GiovanSimone, born in 1479 and Sigismondo born in 1481. But his mother's health at last failed and she died in 1481, possibly from a fall from a horse; it is unclear. Michelangelo was only six years old. This must have caused feelings of loss. We know how deeply

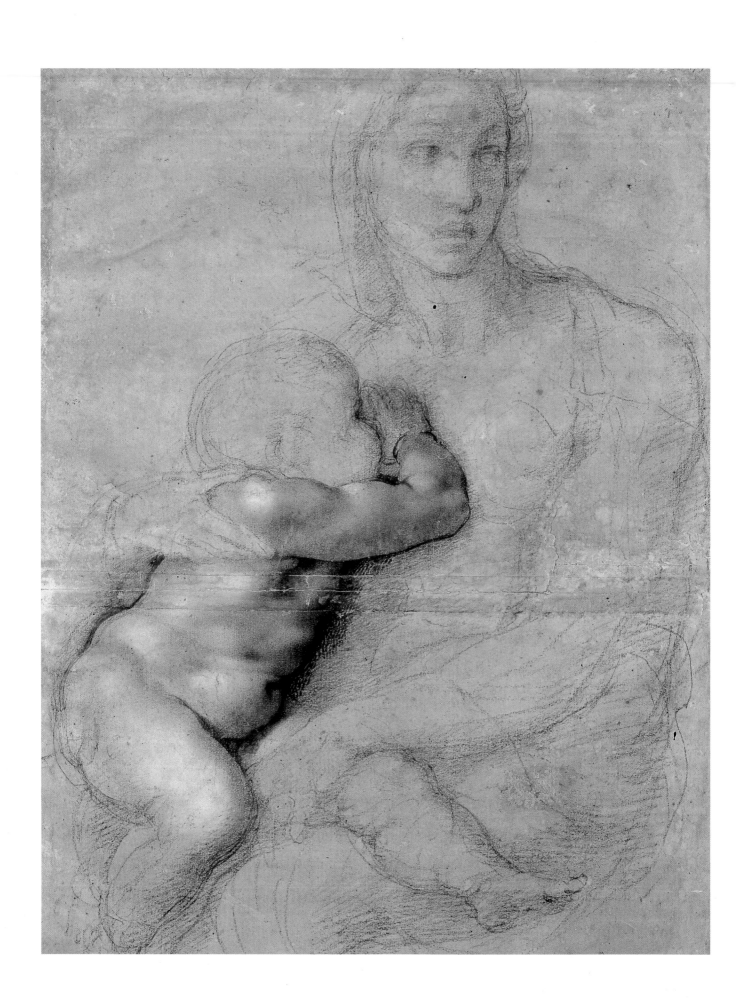

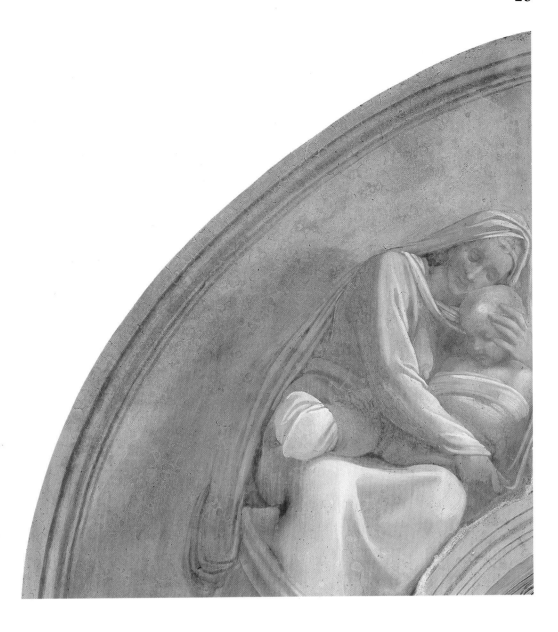

Detail from the lunette of Salmon, Boaz and Obeth.

Michelangelo felt the snubs and rejections by others in later life and it is possible that this early pain and bewilderment affected his adult relationships.

It is interesting that he hardly mentions his mother in the letters to his father (although he does suggest in 1554 to Lionardo, the son of his favourite brother Buonarroto, that he names his new baby Francesca if it is a girl). But his painting and sculpture so often show the subject of mother and son that it must have been very significant for him. When we look at the St Peter's *Pietà*, or at one of the lunettes of the Sistine Chapel ceiling, we cannot fail to be moved by the tender way in which he portrays this deepest relation of child to mother. Art can be a way to understand and organize one's feelings without having to confront them directly, and no doubt this was true for Michelangelo as for other artists.

Four years after Francesca died, when Michelangelo was ten, Lodovico remarried, hoping to create a happier, more unified environment for his young sons in Florence. By all accounts, this

The Madonna and Child, opposite, *a drawing by Michelangelo from the 1520s.*

attempt was not altogether successful, and Michelangelo's return to life with Lodovico and Lucrezia di Antonio Ubaldini da Gagliano in 1485 on the Via dei Bentacordi was gloomy. Life at home was monotonous and despite the exciting street life of the Santa Croce quarter, and his studies in the grammar school of Master Urbino, Michelangelo wanted something else. He was already fascinated by drawing and not very interested in learning Latin and Greek, much to Lodovico's displeasure. Lodovico wanted his second son to follow in the footsteps of his illustrious family, by pursing a career in trade, banking or local government – all highly esteemed in Florence. He could not understand his son's desires or take his artistic vocation seriously. Lodovico had little respect for artists and rejected all Michelangelo's requests to enter a *bottega* (a workshop-studio) where he could learn the trade.

Francesco Granacci, a young friend of Michelangelo, was a pupil and apprentice in the *bottega* of the Ghirlandaio di Currado brothers. Domenico Ghirlandaio (1449-94) was acknowledged by all of Florence to be a master of painting and drawing, and his *bottega* was a hive of activity. Every form of art and craft was practised there, from jewellery-making to oil and fresco painting. In fifteenth-century Florence, the art schools and academies of today did not exist. If a young person wished to learn the trade, he (very rarely she) became apprenticed to a famous artist. A notable exception to this male-dominated system was the sixteenth-century artist Artemisia Gentileschi (1597-1651). She was extremely talented, but she was only able to succeed because she was a student of her own father Orazio (1563-c.1644).

In the *bottega*, in return for a modest wage, the apprentice would help his master in the less important parts of a painting, such as the drapery or architectural features. In this way, the skills and tricks of the trade were handed down from one generation to the next. In 1488, with help from Granacci, Michelangelo at the age of thirteen broke down his father's resistance and Lodovico agreed to allow his son to enter the Ghirlandaio workshop for three years and signed a contract to that effect.

'1488, A record of today, 1st of April, I Lodovico di Lionardo di Buonarroto apprentice my son Michelangelo to Domenico and Davide di Currado for the next three years, with the following agreements, that the said Michelangelo must stay with them to learn to paint and to practise art and shall obey those mentioned above and the aforementioned must give him twenty-four florins in three years; six in the first, eight in the second, ten in the third. In all, the sum of ninety-six lire.'

Below this, in Lodovico's hand:

'Michelangelo has received two gold florins this sixteenth of April and I Lodovico di Lionardo, his father, have received twelve lire, twelve soldi.'

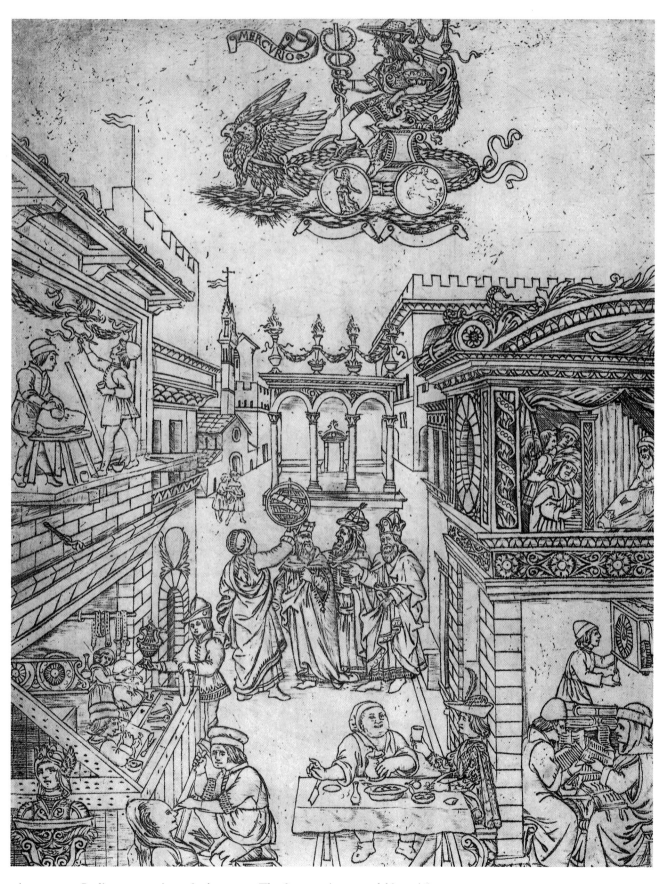

Anonymous Italian engraving of a bottega. The fresco painter and his assistant can be seen in the top left-hand corner.

This is the first record of Lodovico's obsession with money.

The move was a turning point in Michelangelo's life. It gave him the opportunity to spend all his time doing what he loved most – drawing and copying the work of masters of previous generations, such as Giotto and Masaccio. He was also able to witness fresco painting at first hand. He helped the Ghirlandaio brothers on the frescoes at the Church of Santa Maria Novella in Florence. Some scholars believe that there is a male figure that bears his 'signature' in one of the uppermost frescoes. He was certainly responsible for some of the painting on the highest sections of the fresco cycle. Michelangelo loved *torsion* in his figures, which is a twisting tension in a standing position. This is called *contrapposto* in Italian, and is a pose that can be found in antique sculpture.

Michelangelo's study in red chalk for the Libyan Sibyl, 1511. The twisting movement of the figure, clearly observed from a model, probably male, with highly defined musculature, shows Michelangelo's interest in torsion.

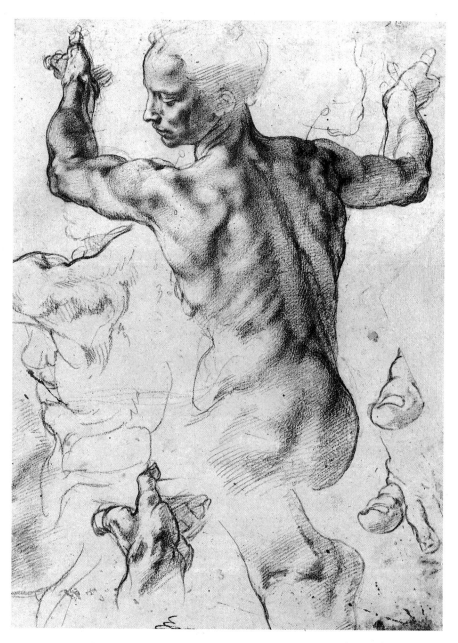

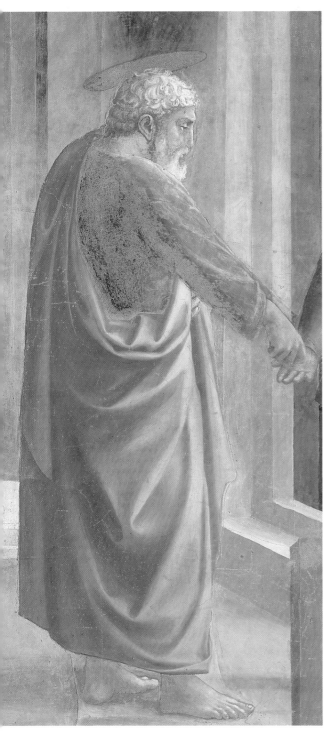

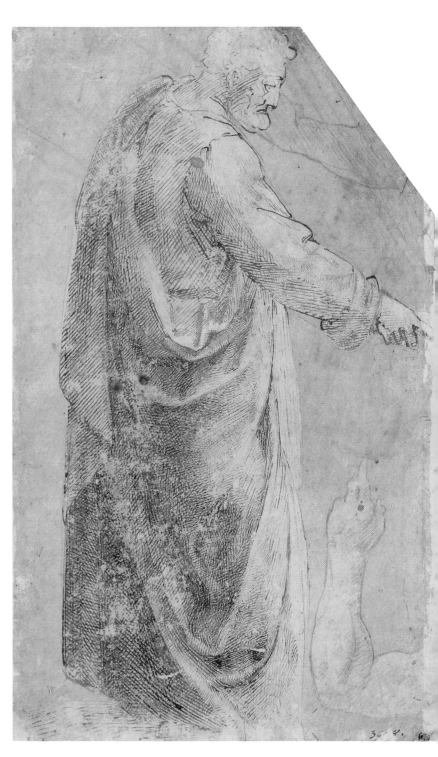

Detail from the recently restored Tribute Money by
Masaccio, c.1427, in the Brancacci Chapel, Santa Maria del
Carmine, Florence, left.

Michelangelo's copy of the same detail. Pen over chalk,
c.1489–90.

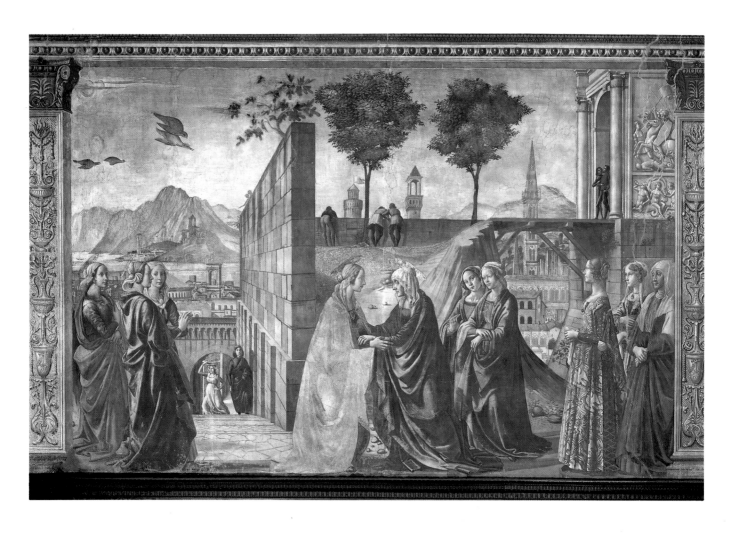

The Visitation *by Ghirlandaio and assistants, c.1491.*

Certainly the influence of this period of work with the Ghirlandaios found its way into his painting on the Sistine Chapel ceiling. Compare the passage of painting of Michelangelo's Cumaean Sibyl's gown and the dress in Ghirlandaio's *Visitation* panel. Michelangelo learned all about colour in their workshop and was able to master the use of *colori cangianti*, shimmering veils of colour which look like shot silk. He became the master of this technique, as is obvious in the Sistine Chapel ceiling, but he had excellent teachers. In later years he must have had cause to be grateful to his first teacher, for it was Domenico Ghirlandaio who taught him the complex skills of fresco painting.

Michelangelo, though, was impatient, greedy for the different experiences that life could offer. He also learned quickly. After only one year, he craved new influences and ideas. In 1489, impatience overtook duty and Michelangelo broke his contract. It was Ghirlandaio himself who introduced him to the Medici, who were the leading family of Florence, and Michelangelo was rapidly drawn into their orbit. They were immensely wealthy bankers and civic leaders and their passion for the arts has become a legend.

The importance of the Medici cannot be overstated. Many

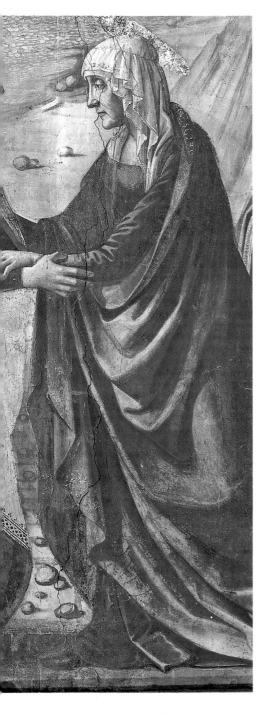

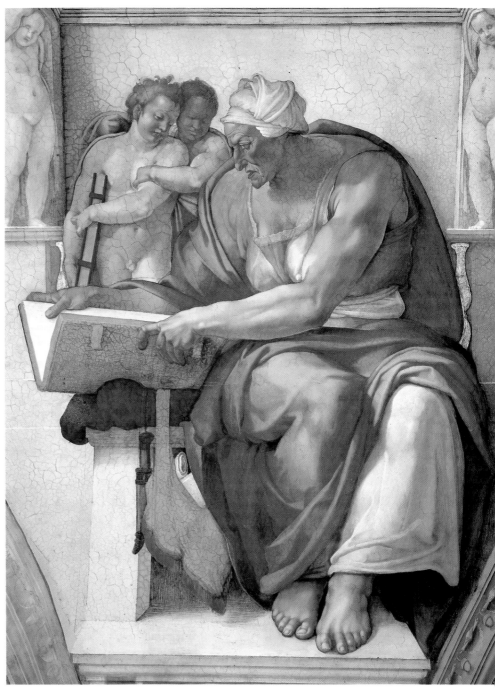

Detail from the Visitation, *showing the sensual handling of colour in the draperies,* left, *and a detail of the Cumaean Sibyl, showing Michelangelo's overlapping washes of brilliant colour.*

great movements of philosophical, social and artistic thought would have died without their patronage and support. The Medici collected many treasures of the past and present and fostered a sense of excitement in Florence. They rebuilt much of the city which had fallen into disrepair over centuries of unrest. They collected ancient manuscripts and brought together the scholars to study them. They created great libraries, and founded what might now be called a museum. The renaissance of the arts almost certainly could not have taken place in the form it did without their dedication and energy.

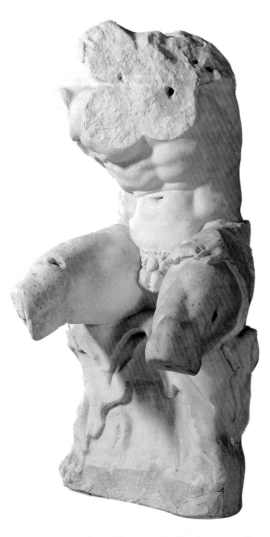

The Belvedere Torso, *Apollonios, son of Nestor, c.50 BC. The twisting forms of this fragment of an ancient statue appealed strongly to Michelangelo.*

Lorenzo de' Medici, who was born in 1449, was the grandson of the first great Medici prince Cosimo, and took over the responsibilities of the family at the age of twenty in 1469. Lorenzo was an extraordinary man, a natural leader, a poet and a person of considerable artistic talent – a rare combination. Michelangelo naturally gravitated towards powerful, older men, as in his relationship with Pope Julius later; and Lorenzo's strength and personality contrasted with the weakness of his own father. Michelangelo was welcomed into the Medici household and Lorenzo treated him as a favoured son.

Lodovico was worried by his son's absorption into the Medici circle. He thought that Michelangelo would end up as a mere *scalpellino*, a stonecutter. A stonecutter indeed! Early works by Michelangelo, sculptures done under Lorenzo's roof, were much more than that. They are mature works of art, uncannily precocious for a boy in his seventeenth year.

Collecting antiquities was an activity that obsessed many a Renaissance prince, and in the garden of his palace near San Marco, Lorenzo had created a sort of small outdoor 'museum' of sculpture. The idea of a public museum is relatively recent, and it is only in modern times that it has become possible to study the art of the past freely in the public collections of great cities. In

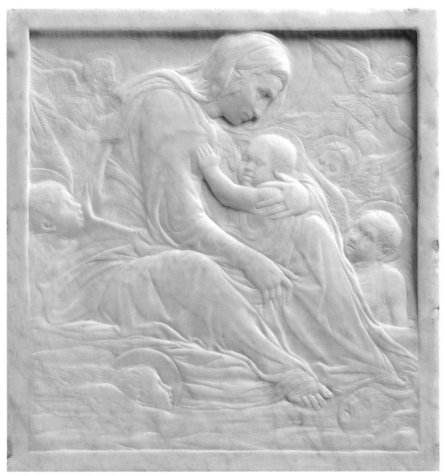

Madonna of the Clouds, *a marble relief by Donatello, c.1425–35. The great fifteenth-century sculptor profoundly influenced Michelangelo.*

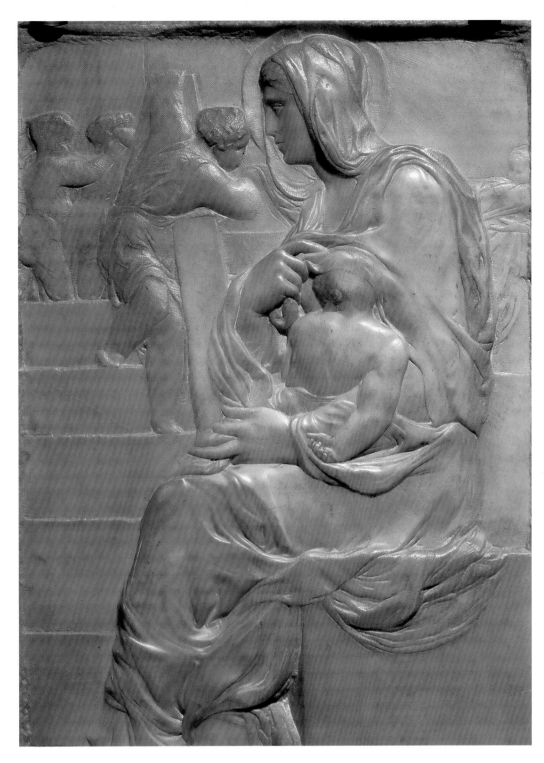

Madonna of the Stairs *by Michelangelo, c.1491–92. Michelangelo was a young man of sixteen when he mastered the technique of Donatello's style of low relief carving,* rilievo schiacciato.

Michelangelo's time, a young sculptor was restricted in his access to the art of the past. Archaeology was scarcely a common pursuit and many of the treasures we now admire were still in the ground, not to be discovered for many centuries. Michelangelo's biographer Vasari describes the formation of a 'school' around Lorenzo's collection, presided over by the elderly sculptor Bertoldo di Giovanni who had been the assistant to the great Florentine sculptor Donatello (c.1386-1466).

Michelangelo lived in the Medici household and spent most of his time in the sculpture garden. He quickly made a favourable impression, creating a small relief carving called the *Madonna of the Stairs* in 1491-92, which owes much to the great Donatello, but is already a masterpiece of originality. It evokes a powerful mother-son relationship with what Nicholas Wadley calls 'bitter-

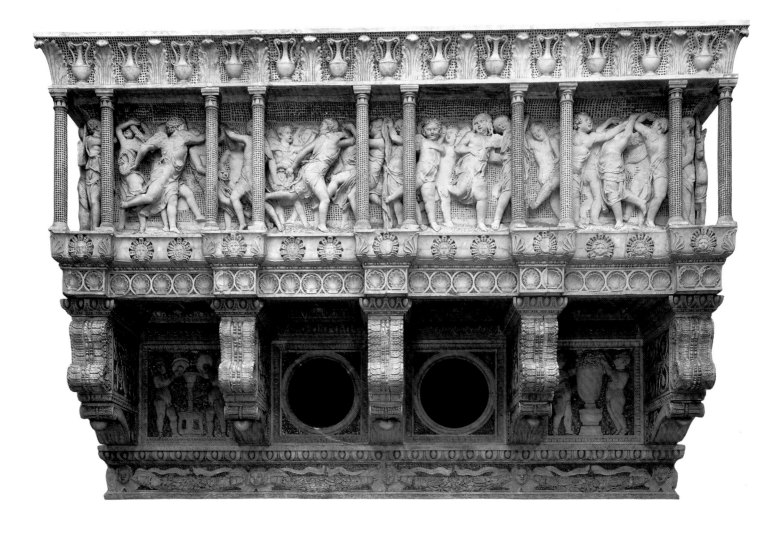

Donatello's Cantoria *(choir gallery), 1433–39. These turbulent little cherubs may have influenced Michelangelo's early sculpture.*

sweet melancholy'. It depicts the lovely Virgin Mary protecting the infant Jesus with tenderness as he nestles at her breast, hidden by her swirling cloak. The intricacy and delicacy of the carving is amazing for a boy of sixteen. Bertoldo and his patron Lorenzo were delighted, which created not a little jealousy amongst Michelangelo's friends. The very different *Battle of the Centaurs* also comes from this period.

Lorenzo's court and sculpture garden were visited by some of the most advanced thinkers of the day. Ideas that are expressed in the design of the Sistine Chapel ceiling can be traced to these early days in Lorenzo's home, listening to the great philosophers of the time arguing about 'Love Divine and Spiritual' and the 'Ideal World'. Michelangelo's imagination must have been fired by the intensity of these philosophical debates about the nature of existence and thought. Important philosophers of the time, Ficino, Poliziano and Pico della Mirandola, were concerned with the relationship of the theories of the pre-Christian Greek philosopher Plato to the Christian concept of a world determined

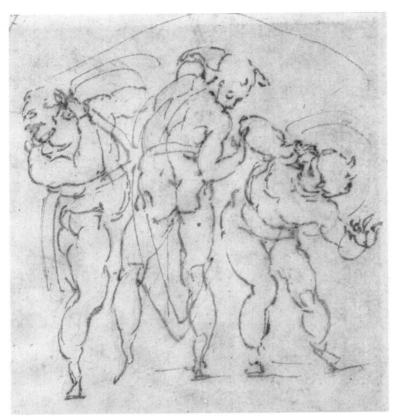

A pen and ink drawing by Michelangelo of three male nudes, probably about 1531. His mature style shows a dynamic handling of this classical theme of twisted, moving forms.

The Battle of the Centaurs, *1491–92, carved by the young Michelangelo in high relief, has had different interpretations. It is thought either to depict a battle between Hercules and the Centaurs, according to Vasari, or the Rape of Deianira with the Battle of the Centaurs (Condivi). Charles de Tolnay attributes the subject to Ovid, describing it as the Rape of Hippodamia. It shows Michelangelo's early preoccupation with the male nude and is influenced by the sarcophagi in Lorenzo's collection. There is little tenderness here, only exhilaration in the massed energy of the struggling warriors.*

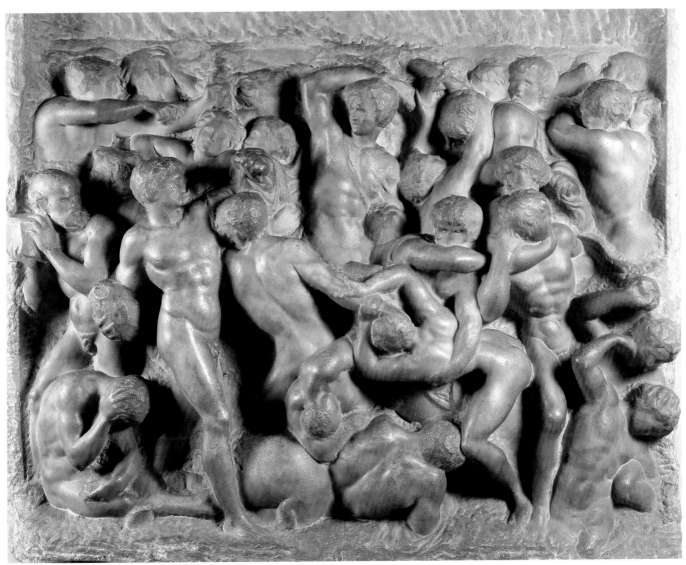

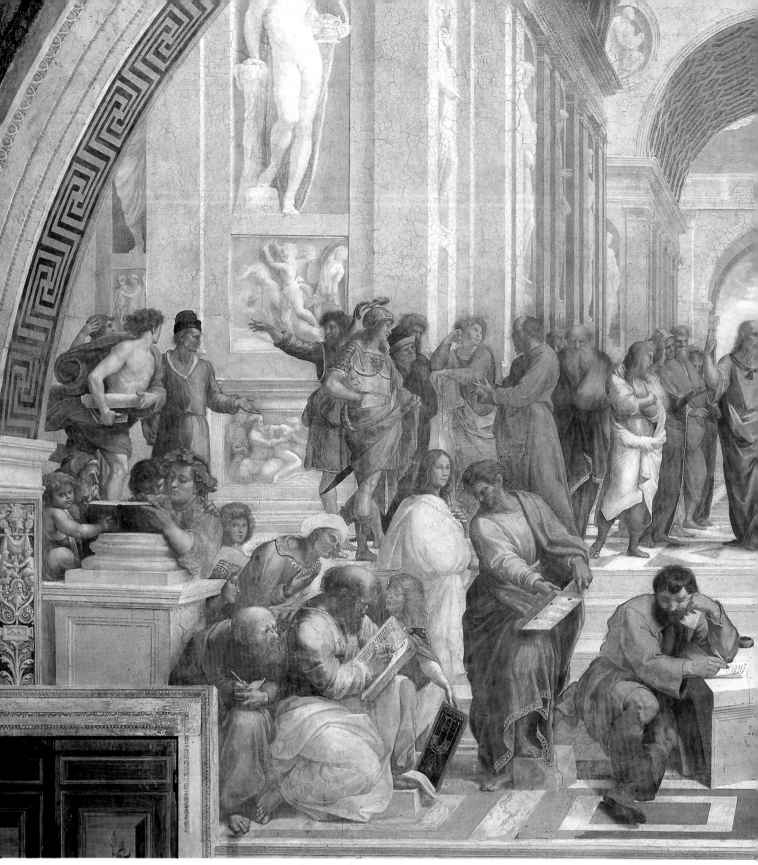

by God, in what came to be known as Neoplatonism. Plato's concept of an 'ideal' world, where knowledge and reason help the development of supreme beauty, was reinterpreted by these men in a Christian context and thus 'New'- or Neo-platonism became the dominant philosophy of the day. An awareness that Michelangelo was familiar with these ideas helps us to understand the often difficult meanings embodied in the Sistine Chapel ceiling.

These carefree days came to an untimely end when Lorenzo

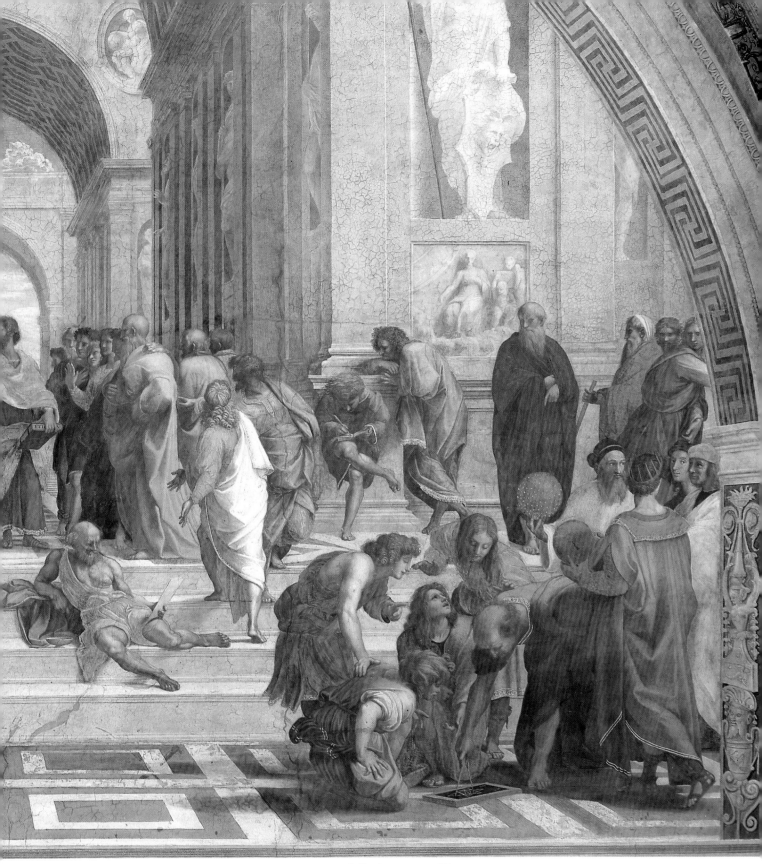

The School of Athens by Raphael, about 1510–12. Stanza della Segnatura. The philosophers of classical Greece are depicted in this large fresco. In the centre is Plato, finger pointing skywards towards the ideal world, holding a copy of the Timaeus. *He bears the unmistakeable features of Leonardo da Vinci. On his left, holding a copy of the* Ethics, *is Aristotle. On Plato's right is the philosopher Socrates wearing a green robe. Sitting lost in contemplation on the steps is a figure in stonecutter's clothes who looks just like Michelangelo. On the lower right of the picture, holding orbs of the heavens and earth respectively, are the astronomer Zoroaster and the geographer Ptolemy. To their right, the youth gazing towards us is a self-portrait by Raphael. The cynic Diogenes sprawls on the steps. The mathematician Pythagoras writes in a book on the lower left of the picture.*

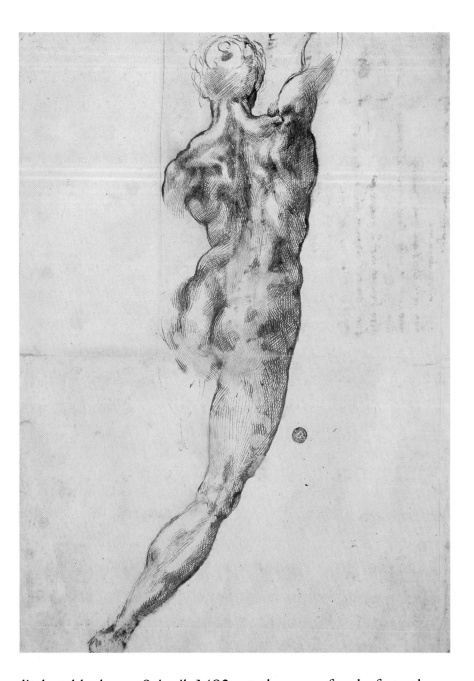

Nude study for the Battle of Cascina *by Michelangelo, c.1504.*

died suddenly on 8 April 1492, at the age of only forty-three. Michelangelo was profoundly affected. His ordered world was destroyed and he became very unhappy. This new experience of death made him intensely conscious of the fragility of life. He turned to the study of human anatomy and was allowed to draw in the mortuary of the hospital of the Monastery of Santo Spirito. In this way he became an expert in the musculature and skeleton of the human body, as is apparent in his obsession with the human figure in both painting and sculpture. For Michelangelo, as for most artists, the understanding of the body was crucial and there were few anatomical textbooks available. His work displays a knowledge of anatomy matched only by that of his contemporary, Leonardo da Vinci.

His depression cannot have been helped by the political and moral climate of Florence at this time. In 1494 the young French king, Charles VIII, invaded the Italian peninsula with a large army, encouraged by certain city states who hoped to see their interests enlarged. At the time Italy was divided into many small, individual, independently governed regions and it did not become a united country until the nineteenth century. The ruler of Florence, Piero de' Medici (1472-1503), lacked the statesmanship and popularity of his father Lorenzo and, in an effort to appease the French, offered to surrender the Medici city of Florence to Charles VIII. Florence was in danger of losing its identity.

In addition to this political threat, there was danger from another quarter. The Dominican friar Girolamo Savonarola had become the Prior of San Marco in 1490, an appointment suggested by Lorenzo. He rapidly became the most powerful personality in Florence, replacing the calmness of Lorenzo's court with hysteria. He was an orator of tremendous dramatic power and his apocalyptic sermons, preached in the main squares of Florence to thousands of people, worked the crowds who heard him into a fever of excitement. He taught that the world was doomed by the great sins of mankind and of the Church. He preached that the population of Florence would die horribly in the fires of Hell if it did not repent of its sins of corruption and

A later drawing by Michelangelo of the Resurrection.

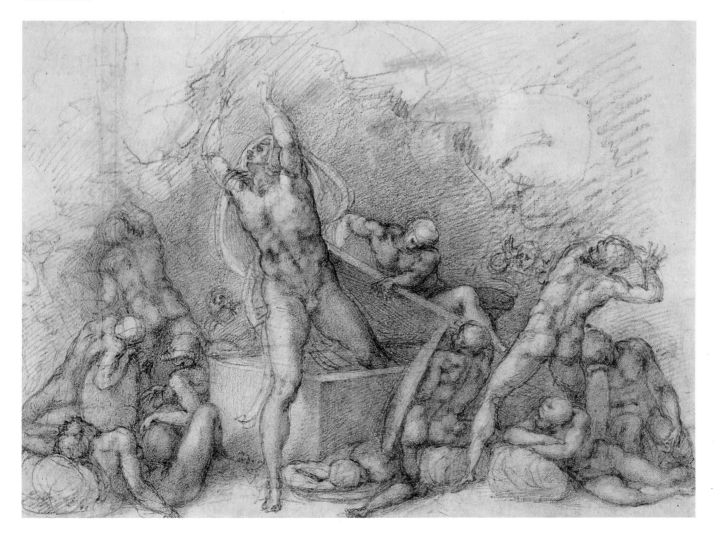

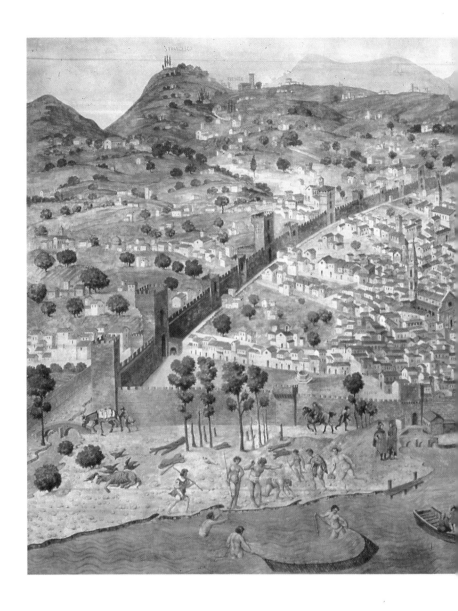

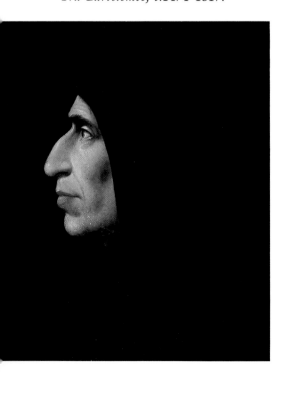

Portrait of Savonarola by Fra Bartolomeo, c.1474–1517.

replace vice with devotion to God. The likely arrival at any moment of the large French army made his prophecy of doom seem only too plausible. He accused the Holy Church with terrifying ferocity and condemned the corrupt priests to eternal hell-fire.

As a young, vulnerable man, Michelangelo was deeply affected by these sermons. He both respected and feared Savonarola. Sixty years later, he complained that he could still hear the ranting voice of Savonarola in his ears. There is no question that Michelangelo's decision to leave his native city owed much to the notorious friar (who was eventually burnt on the cross in 1498). Saddened by the atmosphere around him, and sickened by his older brother Lionardo's adherence to the Savonarolan cause, Michelangelo left Florence in 1494 for Bologna and then Rome. He was to return, but things were never to be the same. New burdens of success and fame were about to be placed on his shoulders.

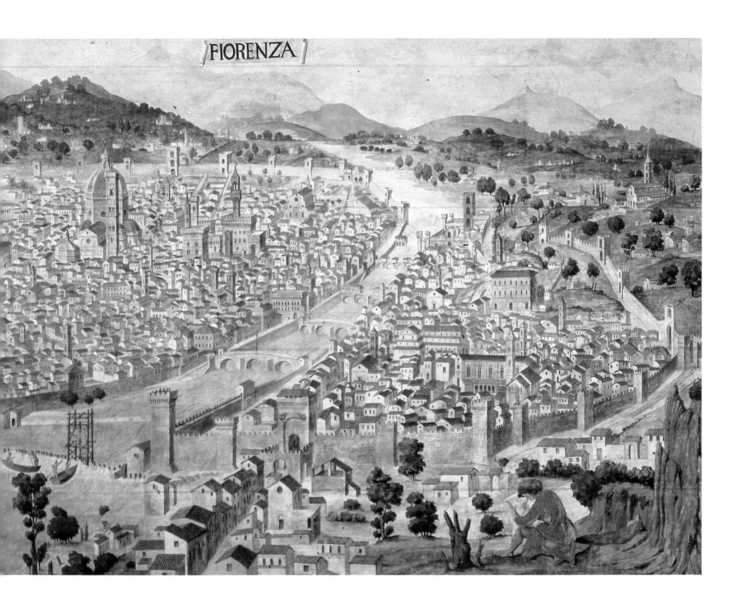

The Catena *map, drawn between 1470 and 1490, shows the size and complexity of Florence at the time of Michelangelo's birth.*

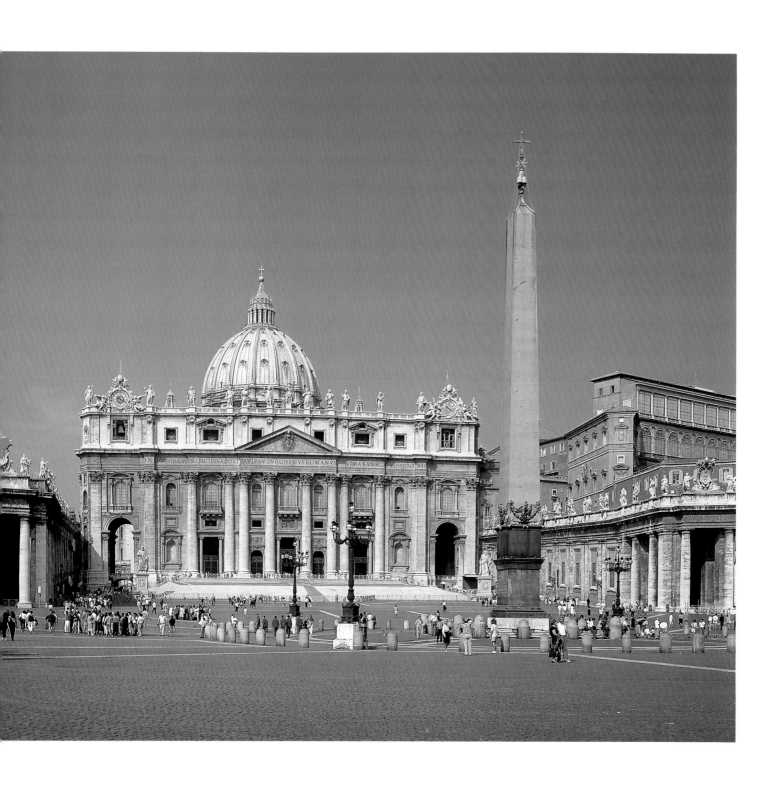

🌿 2 The Commission

In March 1505, Michelangelo, already a famous Florentine artist, was summoned by the Pope to Rome, a call that was ultimately to result in the painting of the Sistine Chapel ceiling. But that was not the original intention.

In order to understand how the sculptor Michelangelo came to paint the Sistine Chapel ceiling, we must consider two themes. The first is the difficult relationship between artist and Pope. This was fraught with misunderstanding, wilfulness and tension. The other is the project for the tomb of Pope Julius II. Michelangelo was brought to Rome in order to glorify the papal reign of this vainglorious man through sculpture, not through painting. It is the tomb which holds the key to the extraordinary history of the Sistine Chapel.

In 1503, the nobly born Cardinal Giuliano della Rovere was elected Pope and formally renamed Julius II. He was sixty years old. His uncle, Sixtus IV, Pope from 1471-84, had in 1473 ordered the building of the Sistine Chapel, which was named in his honour as a solemn witness to his papal reign.

Designed to be the ceremonial centre of the Vatican, the papal city in the centre of Rome, the Sistine Chapel was the site of the election of new Popes in the 'conclave' or meetings of the Cardinals. It was dedicated to the Virgin Mary and High Mass was celebrated in this most holy of places. Built to the specifications of Solomon's Temple mentioned in the Book of Kings in the Bible, the chapel is twice as long as it is high and three times longer than it is wide (40.93 x 20.7 x 13.41 metres, or about 134 x 68 x 44 feet). The Vatican at this time was a cluster of buildings, deliberately set in a position that could easily be defended by the mass fortress of the Castel Sant'Angelo, which still guards its riverside flank. The architecture of the chapel reflects this conscious military purpose. Its stern exterior contrasts starkly with the rich, complex interior, which stands as one of the wonders of the world in its unique celebration of the spiritual and human qualities of mankind. The Sistine Chapel is an important ceremonial centre of the Vatican. But the art within it also directly expresses the spirit of the Italian Renaissance.

Pope Sixtus commissioned some of the greatest artists of the

St Peters, Rome, left *with the Vatican Palace on the right.*

The Sistine Chapel.

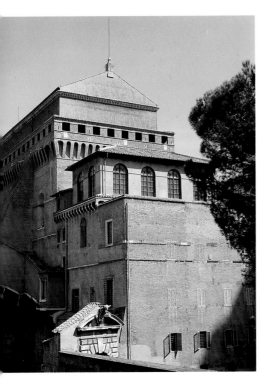

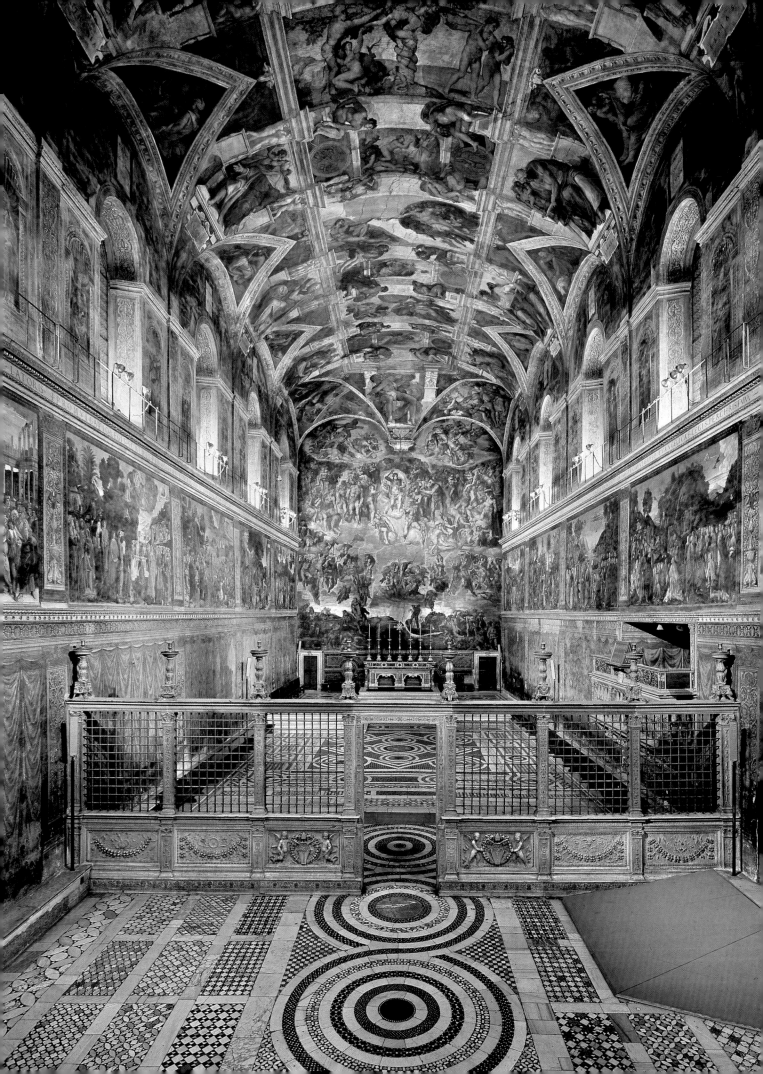

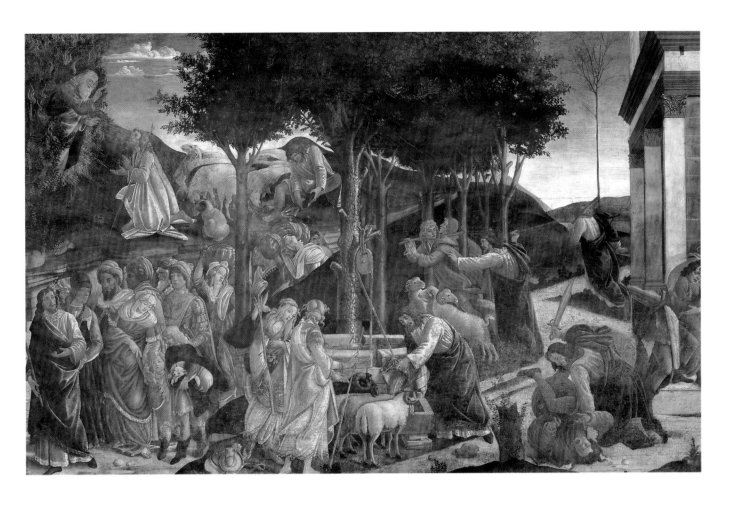

The Youth of Moses *by Sandro Botticelli, 1481–82.*

Interior of the Sistine Chapel, looking west, before restoration.

fifteenth century to decorate the chapel. Among them were Botticelli, Signorelli, Rosselli, Perugino and also Ghirlandaio, Michelangelo's old master.

These earlier paintings on the walls depict scenes from the lives of Moses and of Christ with a liveliness which was reflected in the painting of the ceiling, designed by PierMatteo d'Amelia to look like the vault of the night sky, a heavenly blue speckled with golden stars. Nothing could have been more different from Michelangelo's later reinterpretation of the space.

Upon Julius II's accession to the Papacy, plans were busily made in the Vatican. Julius saw himself as a modern man and wanted to inject the new spirit of the sixteenth century into the Papacy. A warrior Pope, he liked to dress in full military armour and was an active and successful commander of the papal armies. In less than ten years he reasserted the supremacy of Rome as a centre both of the power of the Papal States and for learning and the arts. He was an inspired and imaginative patron and used papal power and money to commission the greatest artists of the Renaissance.

Julius wished to create a monument that would keep his own memory alive for posterity, as the Sistine Chapel had been

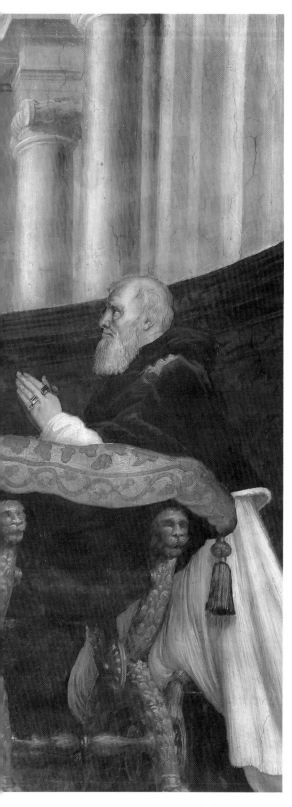

Pope Julius II, detail from the Miracle of the Mass at Bolsena *by Raphael, 1511–12.*

designed to do for his uncle's. What would better commemorate the glories of his life on earth, his conquests, triumphs and piety, than a great tomb to be placed free-standing in the venerable Basilica of St Peter's? This tomb was the commission that Michelangelo embarked upon with barely contained excitement in 1505. A huge monument, approximately 10.5 x 7 metres or $34\frac{1}{2}$ x 23 feet, the tomb would include more than forty statues in complicated arrangements of space. Michelangelo was to be allowed five years to complete this magnificent work and was to be paid 10,000 ducats, which was a good fee.

At the time, Michelangelo was deeply involved in another commission in Florence, the large fresco for the Council Chamber of the Palazzo della Signoria. This fresco was designed to accompany the *Battle of Anghiari* fresco by Leonardo da Vinci, both later abandoned. But he was greatly honoured and excited to be the Pope's choice. There would have been no better project for Michelangelo than that of sculpting the figures and designing Julius's monumental tomb. He was already an established artist, but his reputation rested chiefly on his statues. He was a sculptor on his way to fame and for a young man of thirty, the commission for the tomb was a high honour.

Showing not a trace of uncertainty, Michelangelo left Rome where the project was planned, for the stone quarries of Carrara, bursting with ambitious ideas and enthusiasm. His biographer Ascanio Condivi, writing in 1553, tells us that Michelangelo spent more than eight months in Carrara choosing the marble blocks from which to carve the many figures for the tomb, accompanied only by 'two assistants, his horse and without any other provision except his food'.

With characteristic single-mindedness, Michelangelo responded to the challenge. He concentrated all his creative energies on the project. For Pope Julius, the tomb symbolized his life in the Church and his belief in life after death. For Michelangelo, the tomb would be an eternal monument to his art. He would call out the spirit in the stone and it would live for ever.

What Condivi calls the 'tragedy' of the tomb was a story of obstacles from the beginning. The unwitting creator of these obstacles may well have been Michelangelo himself. Often, his own worst enemy was himself. His plans for the tomb were so grandiose that they may have become an annoyance to the Pope, whose attention became increasingly focused on the much larger project of rebuilding the old Basilica of St Peter's (as it had been known from the time of the first Christian Emperor Constantine) into the magnificent church that stands today. The plans for the new church began to obsess Julius and he became involved with complex drawings for it presented by Donato Bramante, the most

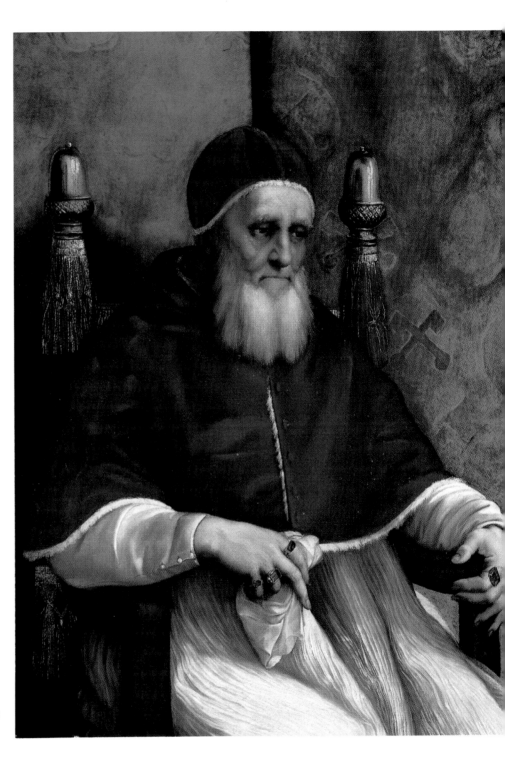

An oil portrait of Pope Julius II by Raphael, 1512.

celebrated architect of his day. Julius spent more time poring over architectural plans than discussing the tomb with his impatient young Florentine sculptor, and in the end refused to lay out any more money for the tomb. Michelangelo was dismissed from the papal court. By May 1506, he was back in Florence, a broken and disappointed man. He writes to Giuliano da Sangallo:

'If I had stayed in Rome, my tomb would be built before the Pope's.'

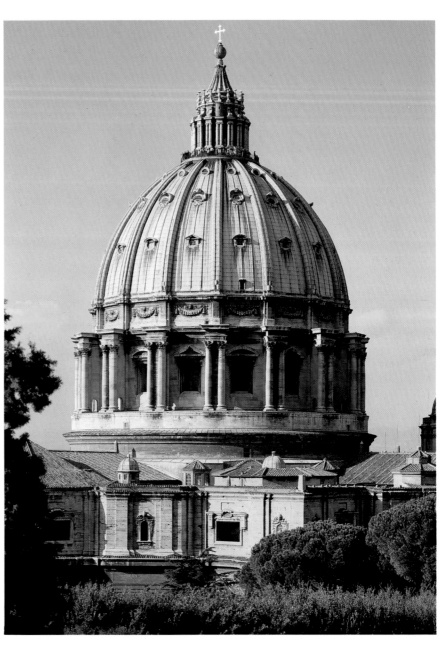

The dome of St Peter's, Rome.

Ironically, the day after Michelangelo left Rome on 18 April 1506, the foundation stone for the new St Peter's was laid. (This new building was not in fact completed until the seventeenth century, long after Julius's death in 1513.) Julius completely lost interest in the original project for the tomb, though Michelangelo remained obsessed with it. The tomb, reduced in scale and importance, was eventually built after much argument with Julius's heirs. It bears no relation to the original magnificent designs. In one sense, however, Michelangelo had the last word on the new St Peter's; he himself was to be the architect of its famous dome some forty years later. He must have greatly enjoyed this revenge on Bramante, who had appeared to replace him in Julius's favour and who thus abruptly turned his life into another quite unforeseen direction.

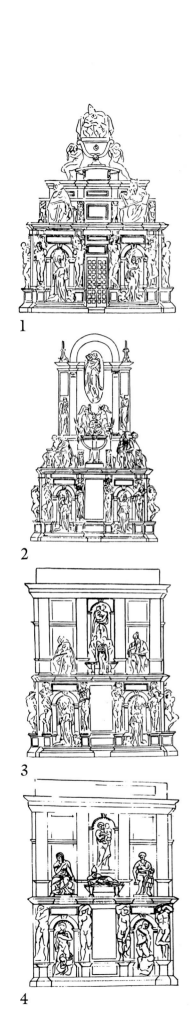

1

2

3

4

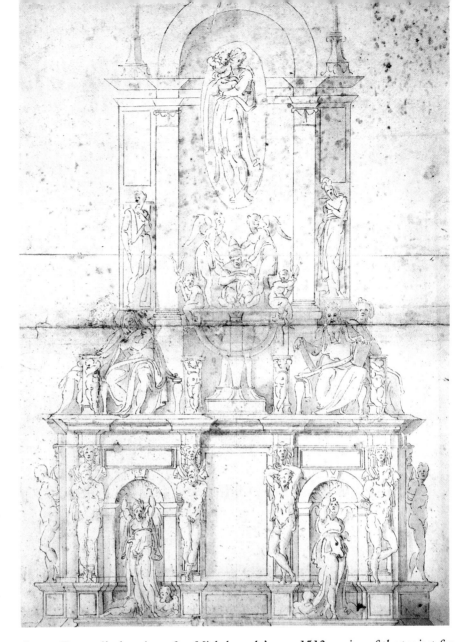

Jacopo Roccetti's drawing after Michelangelo's own 1513 version of the project for the tomb of Pope Julius II.

1 The first project for the tomb of Julius II, 1505.

2 The second project, 1513.

3 The third project, 1516.

4 The fifth project, 1532.

5 The actual tomb in San Pietro in Vincoli.

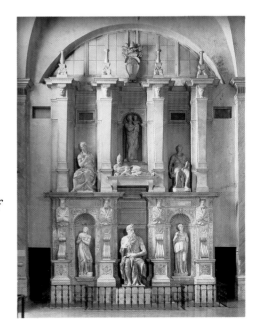

5

Artists are constantly aware of their need for generous patrons, and perhaps there were moments in the difficult years that followed when Michelangelo paused in his labours, high up on the scaffold, and thanked his Pope. But to judge from his letters to his family, his feeling was one of angry disappointment and pain. The story of the Sistine Chapel ceiling sometimes appears to be a tug-of-war between master and servant, though it is obvious now that history has reassigned the role of master to Michelangelo. But Julius's iron will still played a major part in the creation of the ceiling.

The Pope did not want to waste the enormous talents of his young protégé, whom he cared for and respected. Instead of his working on the tomb, Pope Julius wanted Michelangelo to put down his chisels and take up his brushes. The Sistine Chapel needed some refurbishment. It was felt that the original ceiling was old-fashioned and not in keeping with the new spirit of the sixteenth century. The side walls, decorated with scenes from the Old and New Testaments, made the ceiling look too plain, with its simple blue background and golden stars. Someone, it is not known who, had persuaded Julius to have the ceiling repainted. Michelangelo, by papal decree, was chosen for the task in 1508.

It is not known exactly how Michelangelo's name came up when the new project was conceived. There is even the suggestion, of which Condivi gives an account, that Bramante suggested Michelangelo as a suitable candidate for the job in the hope of embarassing his rival. Michelangelo had a reputation as a brilliant sculptor and excellent easel painter, but although he had shown himself an able apprentice in the Ghirlandaio studio in the work at Santa Maria Novella, he had never proved himself as a fresco painter. The *Battle of Cascina* fresco commissioned for the Palazzo della Signoria in Florence had never gone beyond preparatory drawings, although these were considered magnificent. Benvenuto Cellini called the main cartoon the 'school of the world'. It was probably destroyed in 1516, although a complete copy exists by Aristotile da Sangallo and some fragments by Michelangelo remain.

The *Doni Tondo*, painted in 1503-1504, clearly shows his skills as an easel painter. This painting was commissioned by the wealthy Florentine nobleman Angelo Doni as a gift for his wife. It has been cleaned in recent years and in its cleaned state shows off Michelangelo's powerful colour sense, predating the Sistine Chapel ceiling by four years. The brilliant luminosity, and the use of *colori cangianti*, that characterises the painting of the ceiling is already manifestly there in the *Doni Tondo*. This is a crucial point. It negates the argument put forward by critics of the cleaning of the Sistine ceiling that Michelangelo could not understand or manipulate vivid colour in painting. Nevertheless, Michelangelo was desperately unhappy about painting the ceiling, as he had

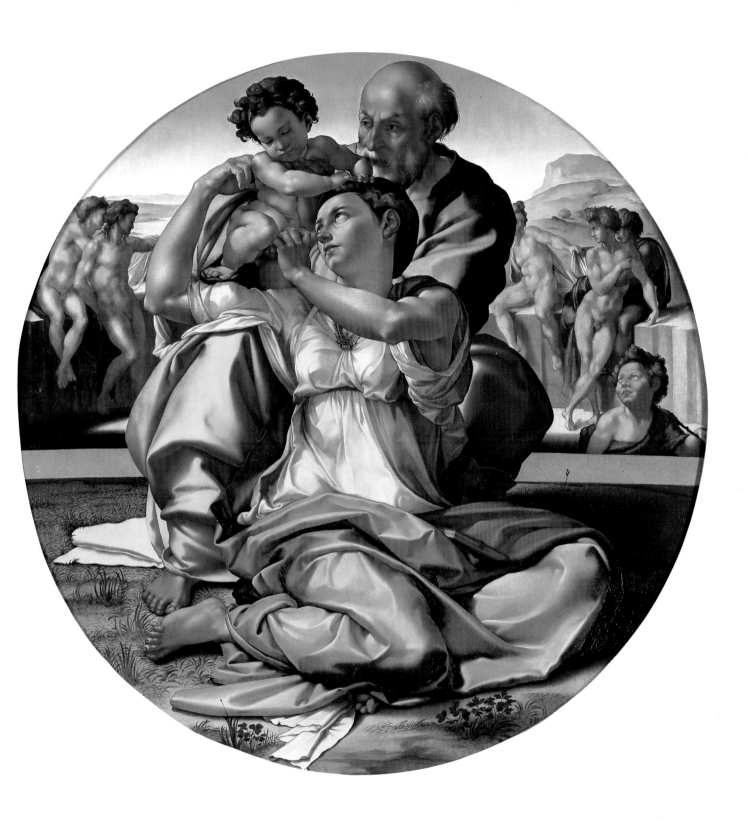

The Doni Tondo *by Michelangelo, 1503–1504.*

already committed himself to the sculptures for the papal tomb. He was in an extremely difficult position. How could he refuse the Pope? He felt that he was the last person in the world to tackle such an enormous job of painting. 'I am a sculptor!' he wrote in a letter at the time. His first and overwhelming loyalty was to sculpture. He was furious, but powerless to change the course of events.

Michelangelo himself was convinced that the whole idea was a conspiracy to make him look a fool so that he should end up making a mess of the job and appear a failure to the Pope. It was an enormous area to cover (40 x 13 metres, or a little more than 131 x 42 feet) and to fail would have been humiliating and embarrassing. His feud with Bramante lasted a lifetime and the circumstances behind the painting of the Sistine Chapel were to be the source of bitterness for many years. They fuelled his bouts of depression and anger at the world. Perhaps the frustration that he suffered gave him the nervous energy required to tackle the Herculean task. It is impossible to create entirely from inspiration alone and artists need a source of inner tension on bad days, when making art just feels like hard work.

In 1508, Michelangelo was summoned back from Florence to Rome after a two-year battle of will. On 10 May 1508, he wrote:

I record that today, May 10 1508, I, Michelangelo sculptor, have received on account from our Holy Lord Pope Julius II five hundred papal ducats counted by Messer Carlino (of the chamber) and Messer Carlo degli Albrizzi, towards the painting of the vault of the Pope Sixtus on which I am beginning to work today, upon the conditions and agreements that appear in the writing of the most reverend Monsignor of Pavia (Francesco Alidosi), and signed in my own hand.

For a fee of 3,000 ducats, Michelangelo contracted to paint the Twelve Apostles on the ceiling. The payments for the work were far from straightforward. They were doled out rarely and in small instalments, so that Michelangelo had terrible problems in paying his expenses. The Apostles were to be seated on thrones, five on each side and one at each end of the chapel. The rest of the Sistine Chapel ceiling would be decorated geometrically in the conventional contemporary manner. However, this plan was soon scrapped. Michelangelo became disenchanted with the designs, saying that: 'It seemed to me that they would turn out poorly'.

He decided that Julius's plan was too banal and simple. The formality of the design would not use his talent for depicting the unclothed human form at all and his powers as an artist would be severely restricted.

It is hard to understand how a man who was initially intimidated by the prospect of painting twelve figures, declaring himself not to be a painter at all, should reject a relatively simple plan and substitute an idea so complex that it had never been attempted before nor ever was again. Why, if he was so unwilling, did he paint more than three hundred figures instead of just twelve? The answer to this question has plagued art historians since Michelangelo's lifetime, and we can only speculate.

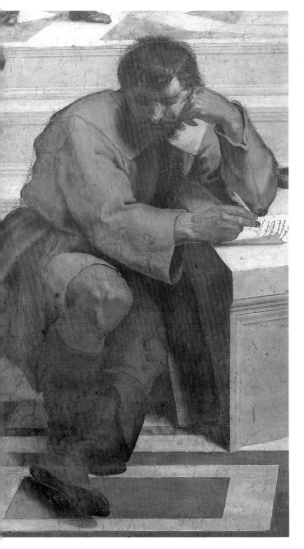

Raphael's portrait of Michelangelo in the School of Athens *(see also pages 34–35).*

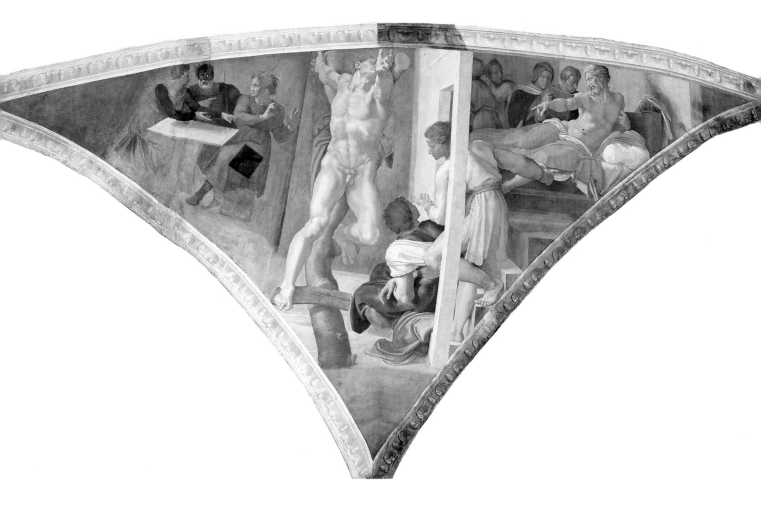

Detail from the spandrel showing the Death of Haman, *marked by tension and vitality (see also page 107).*

It seems obvious when we contemplate the ceiling that someting happened to Michelangelo as he began to tackle this giant task, high up on the scaffold. Perhaps he was merely saying, 'So there!' to his many rivals, and it's as simple as that. Perhaps he was exhilarated by the challenge. He may have come to feel that this much-hated project could harness all the aspirations and contradictions contained within his personality. His disappointment over the tomb project might have built up such a head of steam in him that he needed a creative outlet. All of the energy wasted on the tomb clearly had to find somewhere else to go. His letters and poems reveal him to be an artist fuelled by inner tension, and this tension can be seen in the snap and twist of his painted figures, brimming with vitality and barely contained energy.

But the most compelling answer is even more interesting. It is possible that Michelangelo, a deeply religious and inquiring man, saw intuitively that this would be his opportunity to organize his own personal philosophy. It seems likely that, while painting the ceiling, he underwent a spiritual crisis that was only deepened by the physical pain he suffered. The humorous, self-pitying sonnet written in 1510 to his friend Giovanni da Pistoia is accompanied by the famous caricature (see page 121), showing his contortions as he painted, and details every physical hardship.

52

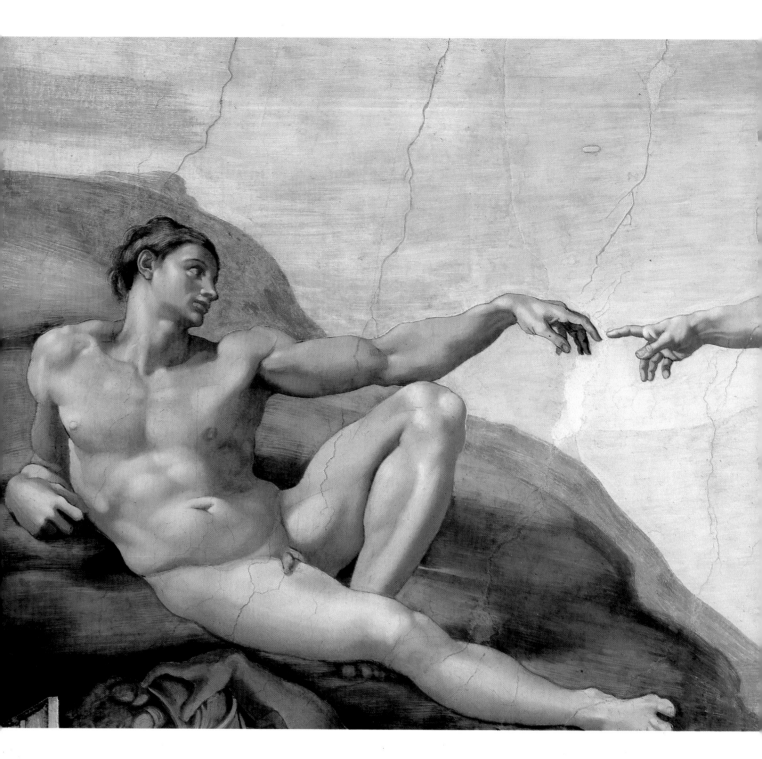

The Creation of Adam.

Michelangelo's spiritual crisis gives the ceiling an intensity that is more than the sum of its parts. There is a compassion for the frailty of our life on earth that is deeply, personally felt. The spectator is moved by a story that takes the Bible only as its point of departure. When Michelangelo revised the earlier plans and began to design a history of Man's beginnings, he left the original idea of the Twelve Apostles a long way behind.

A flash of inspiration electrified his creative energies, very like the invisible charge that passes from God's hand to Adam's in the

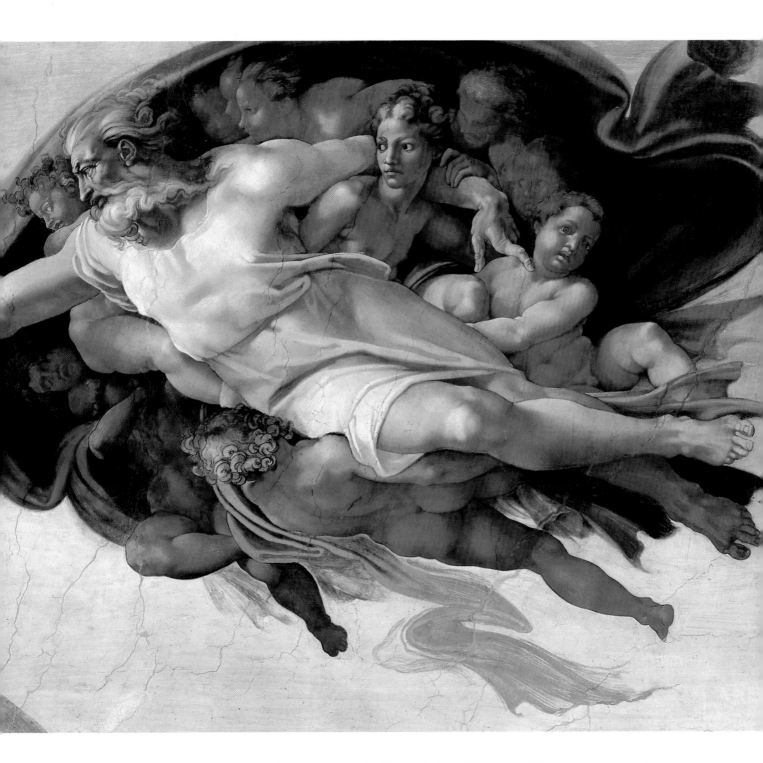

Creation panel. The Sistine Chapel ceiling represents the most complete artistic statement of his belief in the humanity of a loving God and the holiness of human life. Certainly there is no better expression of the spiritual essence of the Renaissance world view in any other artist's work. The Sistine Chapel ceiling could scarcely have been painted at any other time, and by no other artist.

Yet it seems that his grand design was also inspired by more mundane matters. He cannot have ignored the work of artists of the preceding generation who had painted the lower walls of the chapel. There are many theories about the origins of his ideas for the ceiling, which are explained in a later chapter.

Some scholars believe that he designed it alone, using the Neoplatonic ideas from the intellectual Medici circle of his youth. Some believe that he was guided by the learned theologians of the Vatican. But it seems very likely to me that Michelangelo took much of his inspiration from the paintings on the side walls, which he must have admired for their clarity and sharp beauty.

Christ is portrayed as the rightful successor to Moses the law-giver and leader. The foundations of the Catholic Church and the Papacy are depicted in the panel by Perugino which shows the handing over of the keys from Jesus to St Peter, the founder of the Church. Above these panels are portraits of the first sainted Popes, so there is a long and complicated story told with great economy and practicality.

Michelangelo's story ends where these early Sistine Chapel paintings begin. His narrative panels move dramatically from the beginning of the Creation of the World and Man to the Fall from Grace and the emergence of Moses as the new, chosen man. His pictures do not simply relate incidents from the Bible, but are also about the large issues of innocence, sin, punishment and reconciliation. Sure of his point of view, with the Bible as his text, he tells us something timeless about our lives and gives an assurance that there is a meaning behind everything that happens. Whether we belong to an organized religion or not, we are inspired by his passionate belief.

This belief is not only a religious one in the strict sense of the word. Art in its highest form is also an expression of religious feeling and creating art can be a form of worship. As Michelangelo laboured, back bent in the shape of 'a bow from Syria', paint dripping into his face, nagged by an impatient Pope, worried constantly about money and his family, he must have known that the Sistine Chapel ceiling would be his testament to the love of Art as well as to the worship of God.

The entrance and right-hand wall of the Sistine Chapel, facing the altar. On the side wall facing the camera are shown the Last Supper *by Cosimo Rosselli,* Christ Handing Over the Keys *by Perugino, the fifteenth-century Popes St Sixtus and St Felix Romanus, and the lunettes of Azor and Sadoch and Josias, Jeconias and Salathiel. On the entrance wall, to the right of Rosselli's picture, is the* Resurrection of Christ *by Matteo da Lecce and Hendrick van der Broeck (Arrigo Fiammingo).*

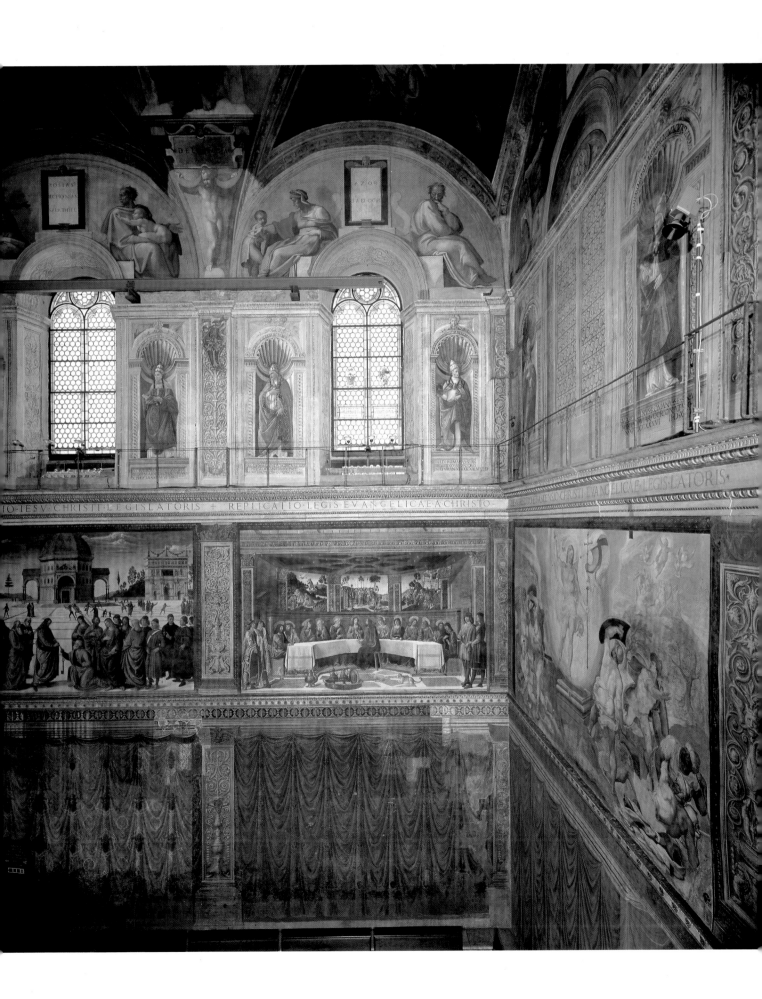

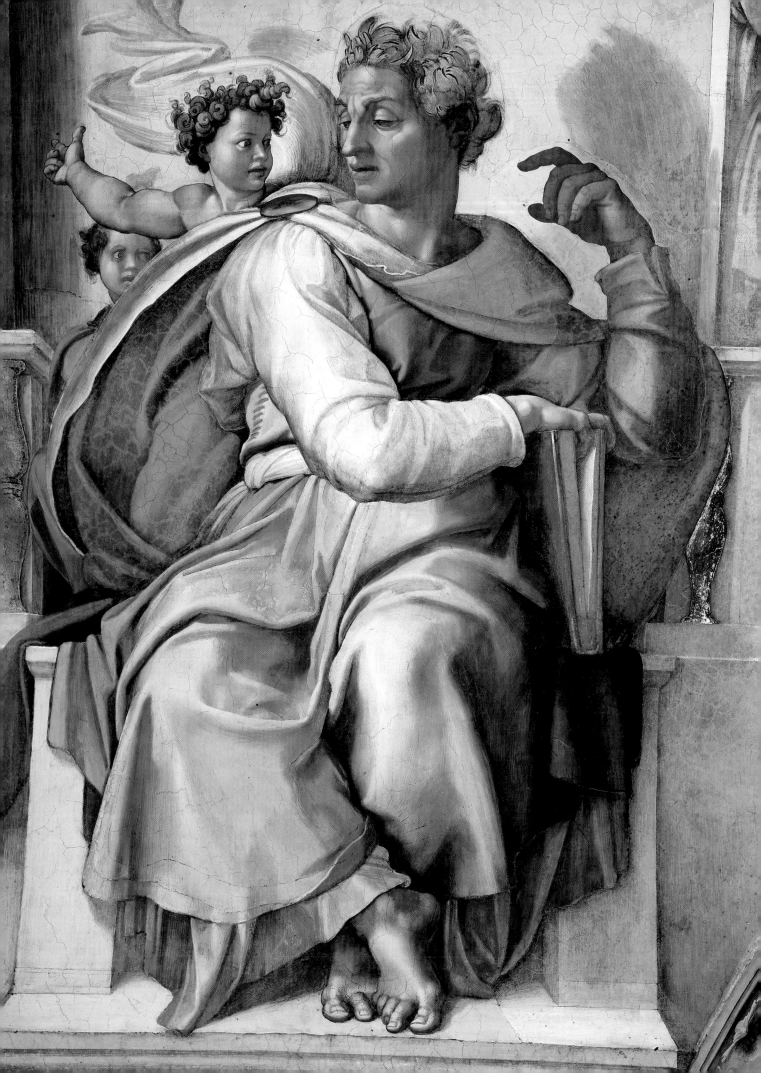

3 The Ceiling

The Sistine Chapel ceiling is a truthful, coherent picture of the world as seen through Michelangelo's eyes. In the twentieth century, we tend to dismiss the importance of art in our society, placing it far below the sciences and technology in the scheme of things. Art seems removed from the concerns of day to day living and is often considered as a pleasant distraction from the jumble and rush of our lives. Few artists' work seems to reflect a coherent world view. Contact with art is literally 'artificial', in the real sense of that word, being seen mostly in museums that are removed from everyday life. We no longer expect artists to reflect a wide-ranging, broadly acceptable picture of the world. There is no common agreement about what the world is like, and the unifying power of religion which prevailed for so long has been greatly reduced.

In the Renaissance, art was woven into the fabric of life primarily through its identification with the Church, as well as in the arts and crafts of daily living. At the time of Michelangelo's work on the Sistine Chapel, artists were esteemed as valued parts of the mechanism that is society. Their work gave spiritual and moral comfort to a wide range of people, because it was an integral part of religious life. The Church was at the centre of Renaissance culture in Italy. During religious services, the congregation could gaze on magnificent painted altarpieces and frescoed ceilings. The vision of great artists nourished the vision of the faithful. The Church, that greatest of patrons, provided countless artists with a livelihood, while giving the congregation images to look at during the long Mass.

The artist used the rich stories of the Bible to give a sense of meaning to the moral code laid down by the Church. The worshippers, lay as well as clergy, who were tempted to disregard the commandments sent down from God to the people of Moses, had only to look up, for example, at the dreadful shame on the face of the banished Adam in the Sistine Chapel, to see the consequence of disobedience. A sermon on the wickedness of the sins of the flesh could be amply illustrated by looking up at the *Drunkenness of Noah*. Religion and art were linked together by a common goal: to serve the glory of God and celebrate the

The Prophet Isaiah.

58

complex beauty of His creation. So artists held a powerful position in society. Their job was to reveal the message contained within the Scriptures – that through faith Man could be redeemed. In His great goodness, God would forgive Man's sins, and all might be saved.

Michelangelo completely believed in this message. That he was a very religious man is apparent as much in his poems and letters as in his art. The explanations of his faith were completely satisfactory to him. For him and his contemporaries the history of Man's origins, as told in the Bible, was a wholly credible story. Today it is hard for many people to trust such unity and to give themselves over to the completeness of Michelangelo's vision.

The Sistine Chapel ceiling is the expression of a world with well-defined edges. In its own creation, it celebrates the creation of the world by a benevolent but strict God. Those who view it must allow themselves to be embraced by Michelangelo's vision of God's protective love and forgiveness. He wants us to realize that our lives depend on God's wisdom and mercy. Preconceptions and prejudices must be cast aside to understand the true nature of the ceiling. We must try to accept Michelangelo on his own terms.

Even in his own time Michelangelo was a legend. His difficult personality and struggles with his own inspiration have since elevated his life to the status of myth. He was already mythologized by his admirer and biographer Vasari, who was responsible for the phrase *Il Divino Michelangelo*. His fame was extraordinary. In our culture, there is no equivalent. He was not known to his public by appearance. Moreover, only the educated and well-born of society would have had access to much of his work. Unlike art of the Early Renaissance, much of the painting of this period, such as the Sistine Chapel, was not on public display.

His work has provided inspiration for thousands of others, and many a scholarly career has been built on different interpretations of the meaning behind his work, which I describe in the next chapter. It is a sign of its richness that it has inspired so many thinkers. Because the ceiling is hard to look at physically (viewers must crane their necks backwards in order to take in the 550 square metres of painting, nearly 6000 square feet, twenty metres or about sixty-five feet above their heads), it is therefore thought necessarily to be difficult from an intellectual point of view. The subject matter, its iconography, can seem difficult, but the painting on the ceiling can be read on many levels.

One of its most interesting aspects is the problem of perspective. We know from experience that reality is full of movement. With the development of the mathematical system of perspective in the fifteenth century (devised mainly by Brunelleschi and Piero della Francesca), artists were able to imitate the

A scene from the Life of St Francis *by Giotto, c.1297–1305 (see also page 14).*

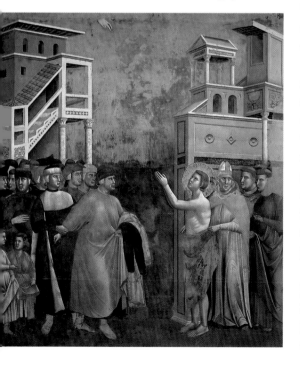

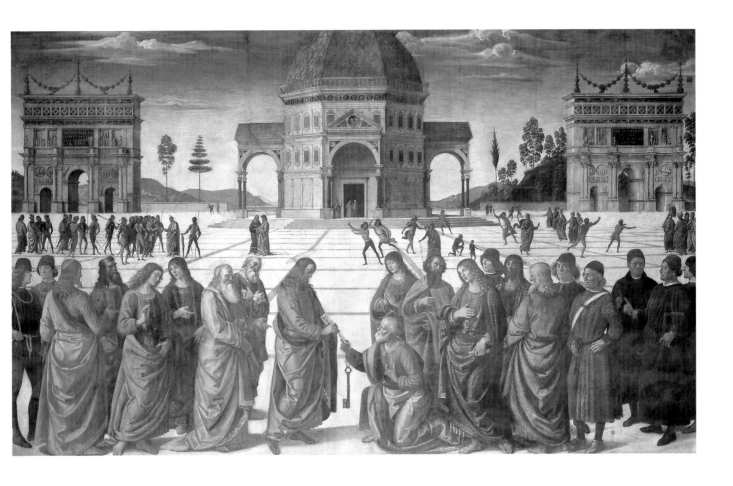

Christ Handing Over the Keys *by Perugino, one of the paintings on the side wall of the Sistine Chapel, (1481-2).*

reality of the physical world in their art, through a form of geometry. This can be seen even as early as the beginning of the fourteenth century in the work of Giotto (see page 14 and opposite).

The basis of the system is that parallel lines appear to converge at a point on the horizon (the vanishing point), as can be seen when you look down a railway track or along a straight road. Figures appear larger as they come closer to the viewer and smaller as they retreat. In this system, figures seemed to be placed in a three-dimensional world with depth. Paintings became windows on to the real world. They became more realistic and the space inside the paintings appears infinite and full of possibilities. Perugino's painting of *Christ Handing Over the Keys*, from the earlier epoch of the Sistine Chapel, which was very important to Michelangelo, illustrates the new perspective very well. Our eyes are drawn into the lively world of his painting by perspectival devices such as the grid of lines of the flagstones of the square behind the main figures. The main action seems to be happening close to us, because the nearer figures are larger and more important than the little figures running about in the middle distance. So we feel part of the scene and at ease and involved.

Michelangelo works differently in his ceiling. His decision to create a world of constantly shifting perspectives is deliberate. He

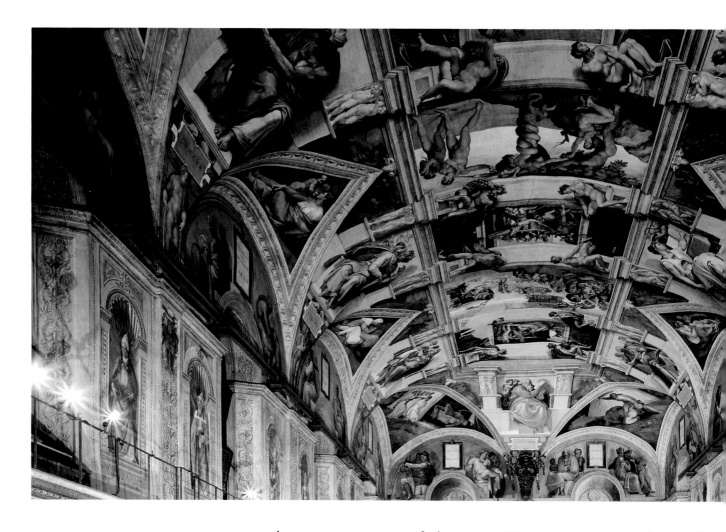

does not want us to feel at ease. His perspective stretches and pulls and folds in upon itself. The first impression – so very important – is of movement. The figures arching above our heads seem to threaten to pull down the ceiling with their weight. An energy radiates downwards from the vault and we grow tense with the strain of making sense of the space and forms. The sensation is overwhelming. We want to be able to 'read' the ceiling, to make a coherent story in our minds. We cannot do this easily. The main elements of the story are painted in different perspectives. The narrative panels, which alternate between large and small, look like paintings hung between the fictive or false beams of the ceiling, making a story as you walk down the chapel away from the altar towards the east door, which was the original entrance. On the other hand, the Prophets and Sibyls have a greater illusion of reality, appearing actually to be seated on thrones along the curved sides of the ceiling. It is as if they had climbed out of the panels and taken up residence around the walls.

Our eyes must work extremely hard to see the whole of Michelangelo's world at the same time. He wants us to work and insists that we do. He does not want us to feel complacent or comfortable or to relax into a sense of peace and contentment. Just as his sculptured figures seem to explode out of the marble that imprisons them ('Even the greatest artist has no idea that is not already buried deep within the stone,' he says in his sonnet for Vittoria Colonna, which is translated on page 134 in this book) Michelangelo's painting wants to burst its two-dimensional shackles. The serene realism of the earlier generation's work, seen in the side-wall paintings, has been respectfully and lovingly rejected. In its masterly way, the Sistine Chapel ceiling is the most revolutionary piece of painting since Man first painted his hunting conquests on a cave wall.

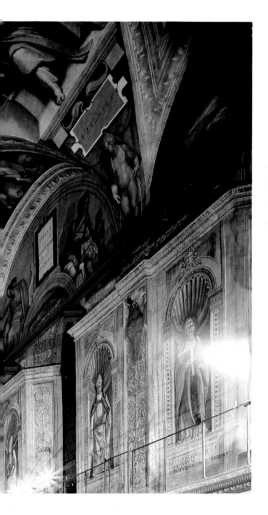

The design of the Sistine Chapel ceiling does not make for easy viewing.

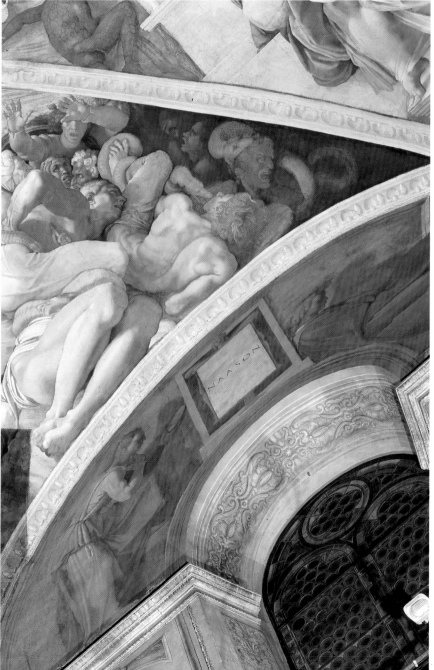

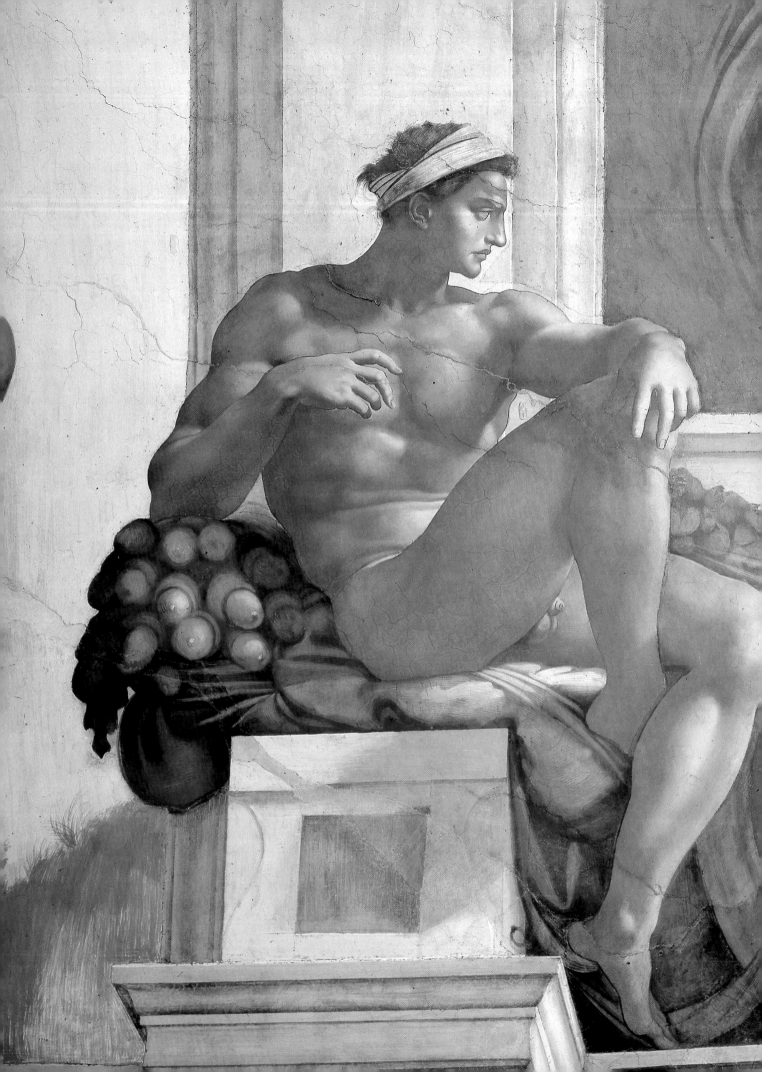

4 Understanding the Image

Among the many theories proposed by scholars, there are six that seem to me to be the most illuminating. A brief look at them can help in understanding Michelangelo's work, though it seems unlikely that the Sistine Chapel ceiling really represents the complex and rarified series of codes that some of the experts would have us believe. Michelangelo was an artist above all else, though a very well educated one. To him, an artist rather than an intellectual, the work was important chiefly for its visual impact, no matter how rich in meanings.

The controversy that has smouldered over the centuries about the authorship of his ideas is ultimately irrelevant. In the debate over whether the ceiling was inspired by the learned Vatican theologians or the Neoplatonic philosophers, the power and punch of Michelangelo can be completely lost. Why can we not take him at his own word when he declares in a letter to his friend Fatucci, in 1508, that having rejected the original, boring scheme (of the Twelve Apostles) he is being allowed by Pope Julius to 'do whatever I wanted' (*'quello che io volevo'*)? Why not give him at least some credit for the authorship of his own work? Certainly he was guided in the organisation of his ideas and certainly their coherence is unlikely to have been totally his own. The Dominican theologians were powerful exponents of religious dogma and the Sistine Chapel *was* the most important chapel in the Vatican, being the site of the Conclave. But it was Michelangelo's hand that painted the ceiling.

The different interpretations of the ceiling attempt to explain some very strange juxtapositions of the pictures. Although the central panels tell the story of Genesis, the story is not always told in sequence, and other non Judaeo-Christian elements are brought in. The figures of the Prophets and Sibyls have no place in the Genesis story and their relevance is a heated issue. The twenty male figures that enclose the Genesis panels, the *ignudi*, are mysterious too. They are placed in such a way that they seem to serve a function beyond pure decorativeness, although their formal function is clear. They help the eye make the transition from the perspective of the narrative panels to the illusionistic style of the fictive architecture. They serve as a kind of visual

Ignudo, *between the* Division of Light from Darkness *and the* Creation of the Sun and Moon.

64

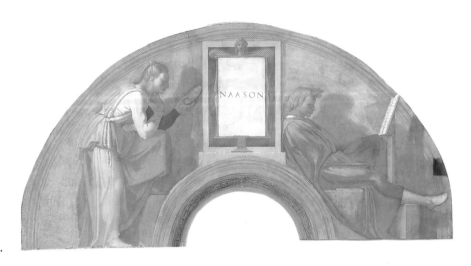

The lunette of Naason.

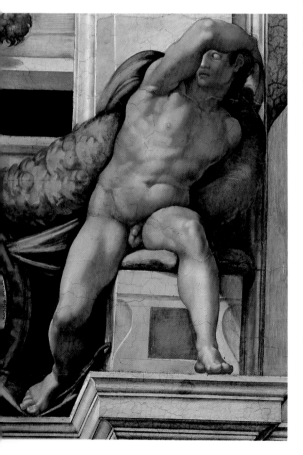

Ignudo, *between the* Creation of Adam *and the* Creation of Eve.

'bridge', but are clearly much more than this. The lunettes and small triangular spandrels above the windows depict the ancestors of Christ, but also appear to have a meaning that goes beyond the telling of the biblical story. These are the kinds of puzzles that have vexed scholars over the centuries.

1. The Neoplatonic view

This suggests that the ceiling is the visual expression of the Neoplatonic school of philosophy, familiar to Michelangelo from his early youth in Lorenzo de' Medici's household. The Ideal World, articulated by the Greek philosopher Plato, in which Beauty is created through Reason, is fused by the Neoplatonists with the Christian belief that the ultimate reason is God. This view explains the *ignudi* as embodiments of ideal male beauty, while at the same time seeing them in the Christian tradition as angels without wings, bound by their solid flesh to earth, but capable of escaping their mortal bonds.

2. The Christian Doctrinal View

It is asserted that Michelangelo adopted complex theological dogma to create his programme of painting, using symbolism derived from both the Old and New Testaments, from St Augustine, and from the hell-fire sermons of Savonarola. To this end we must assume great familiarity not only with the Bible but also with many of the more complex interpretations of it. This view would explain the Prophet Jonah, for example, as a kind of 'sign' for Christ, with Jonah's time in the belly of the whale linked with Christ's time in the 'belly' of the sepulchre.

3. The Structural View

Here the ceiling is seen as a symbolic structure, where placement is all-important. In Michelangelo's time, the Sistine Chapel was

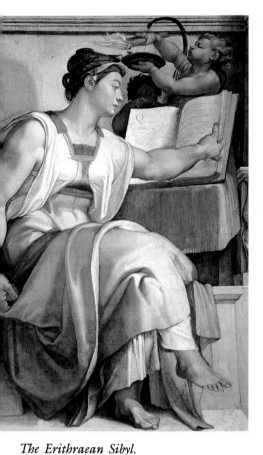

The Erithraean Sibyl.

A detail from Perugino's Christ Handing Over the Keys *showing the Arch of Constantine.*

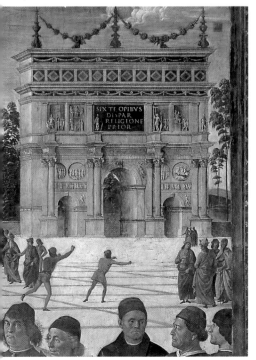

divided into two separate areas, the presbytery and the lay part, separated by a marble screen rising from the floor. The presbytery, where the important personages of the Church, such as the Cardinals, were seated, was near to the high altar under the four panels which contain the images of God. Thus the goodness of God is identified with His ministers on earth.

The structural viewpoint also incorporates the placement of the Prophets and Sibyls and attempts to explain their physical situation. For example the Erithraean Sibyl, according to legend, married Noah's son and therefore sits next to the panel depicting *Noah's Sacrifice.*

4. The Art-Historical View

There are two aspects to this theory. One is centred on the chapel itself, relating to the fifteenth-century wall paintings, which depict the laws of Moses and of Christ – 'under law and under grace' (*sub legem et sub gratia*). The conclusion is that Michelangelo wanted to describe the events in human history before the law was brought down by Moses and before Grace, represented by Christ. The walls and ceiling of the Sistine Chapel would thus tell the whole tale, from Man's beginnings in Genesis to the earlier paintings from the Old and New Testament that describe the leadership of Moses and of Christ.

Other scholars have chosen to see the Sistine Chapel as a substitution for the abandoned tomb of Pope Julius. They have analysed the ceiling as the project of a frustrated sculptor. It is seen as an opened-out tomb, with the three dimensions of architecture and sculpture flattened out like a collapsed box. This explains the false or 'fictive' architectural features, such as the cornices and thrones. There is an interesting similarity between the *Bound Slaves* planned for the tomb and the *ignudi* of the ceiling.

5. The Architectural View

The Perugino painting of *Christ Handing Over the Keys* was a major, formative influence on Michelangelo. The peculiar double image of the Arch of Constantine in the painting, coupled with a familiarity with the actual arch which stands at the entrance to the Roman Forum, seems to have given Michelangelo several crucial ideas. The figures in niches, the medallions and the cornices in the Roman arch appear to have contributed to the painted architecture of the ceiling. Michelangelo's disguising of the barrel vault is brilliant and foreshadows his later, very successful career as an architect. It is impossible to determine where the 'real' architecture of the vault stops and the 'fictive' architecture of the painting begins.

6. The Renaissance World View

An important aspect of the Renaissance period is a fascination with the past and an urge to collect trophies from antiquity. The fusion of antiquity with contemporary Renaissance life promoted the happy idea that Man was timeless. In the ceiling the antique elements, the Sibyls who predicted the future before the coming of Christ, and the Christian Prophets, who predicted that mankind would be redeemed by the Saviour, are joined together. Christian morality and pagan soothsaying are given equal importance by Michelangelo. The element of Time is thus injected into the element of Space, creating the kind of unity beloved of the ancients.

The Persian Sibyl, left, *and the Prophet Joel.*

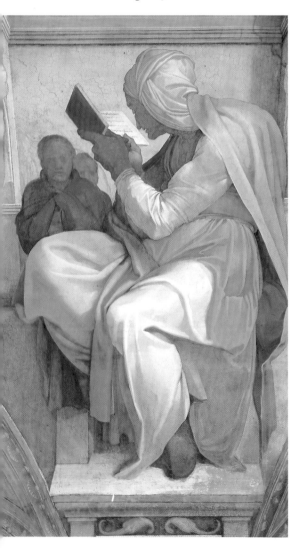
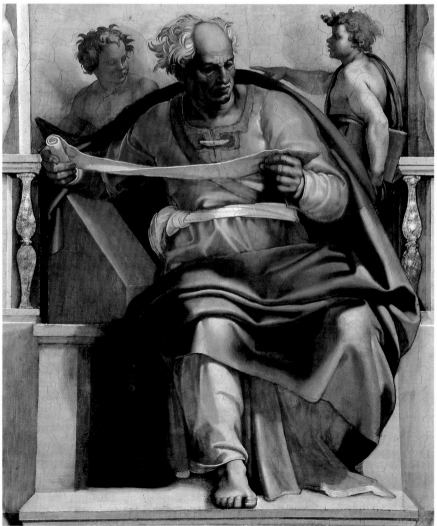

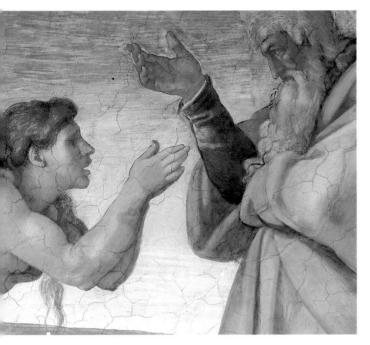 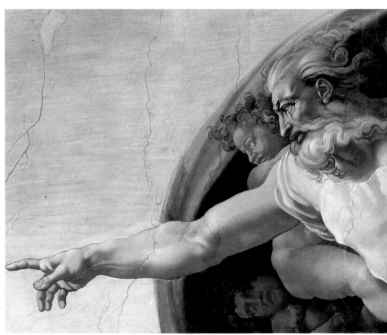

Detail, left, *from the* Creation of Eve *and*, right, *the* Creation of Adam.

All these theories contain truths about Michelangelo's work and they can help to further our understanding of his work in the Sistine Chapel. A great work of art is like a kaleidoscope. The patterns inside continually shift and merge according to the way we look at them. Over the four years of Michelangelo's life that were dominated by this great cycle of painting, even *he* may sometimes have lost sight of his original intentions.

One thing is clear. There is a distinct change in scale, style and feeling halfway across the ceiling. Why is this? Is it because Michelangelo had by then truly mastered the skills of fresco painting? Is it because his financial problems with the Pope – always a source of friction – were relatively resolved? Or is it because some time in late 1510, possibly early 1511 (it is unclear from the documents), the complicated arrangement of scaffolding was moved, enabling Michelangelo to gaze upon the work he had done so far for the first time since late summer 1508?

The midway point (and we must remember that Michelangelo worked in reverse order of the Genesis story, ending up in 1512 over the altar with the *Division of Light from Darkness*) is the panel depicting the *Creation of Eve*. It seems obvious, even to the untrained eye, that the painting becomes more monumental and more direct after that point. In the *Creation of Eve* God is a Renaissance man, stern and wise. He stands like a priest. In the *Creation of Adam* He is mythic, supernatural, a cosmic force. He dives through the heavens. The Prophets and the Sibyls, as well as being considerably larger in the second half, are much more expressive. The difference between the Prophet Zecchariah sitting sedately on his throne at one end of the chapel and the explosive,

Jonah, left, *and the Prophet Zecchariah.*

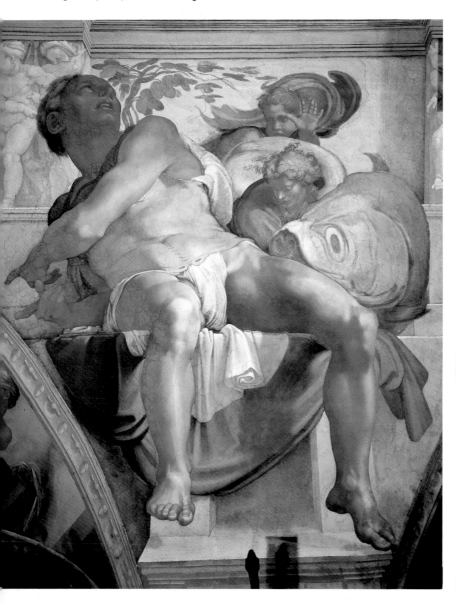
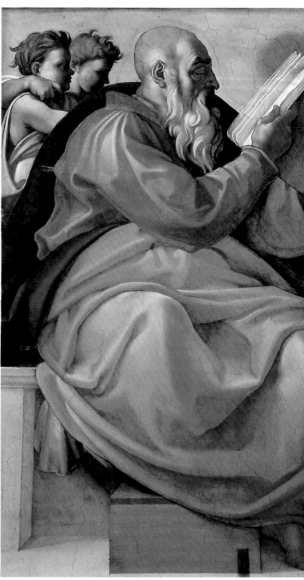

twisted form of Jonah at the other is extraordinary. It seems to me that Michelangelo is responding to his own creation. The experience of looking at his own work, and of painting it, has changed him.

5 The Iconography of the Ceiling

The Narrative Panels

The central spine of the Sistine Chapel ceiling is composed of nine horizontal panels of varying size, depicting scenes from the Old Testament. The first three panels which are near the altar at the western end show the Creation of the World by God. The next three panels illustrate the Creation of Adam and Eve and their fall from grace in the Garden of Eden. The last three panels tell the story of Noah and events in his life. Michelangelo painted these in reverse order, starting with the *Drunkenness of Noah*. These narrative panels are surrounded by many complicated stories and images taken mostly from the Bible, but also from classical mythology. I have chosen to make detailed comments about an example from each type of image, chosen for their representativeness, visual clarity and power.

The Division of Light from Darkness

And God said, Let there be light; and there was light. And God saw the light that it was good; and God divided the light from the darkness. (Genesis I, 3-5)

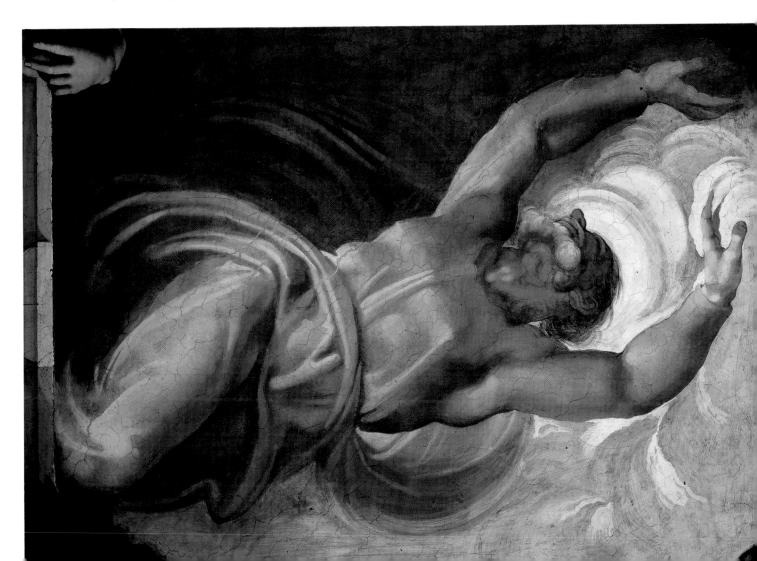

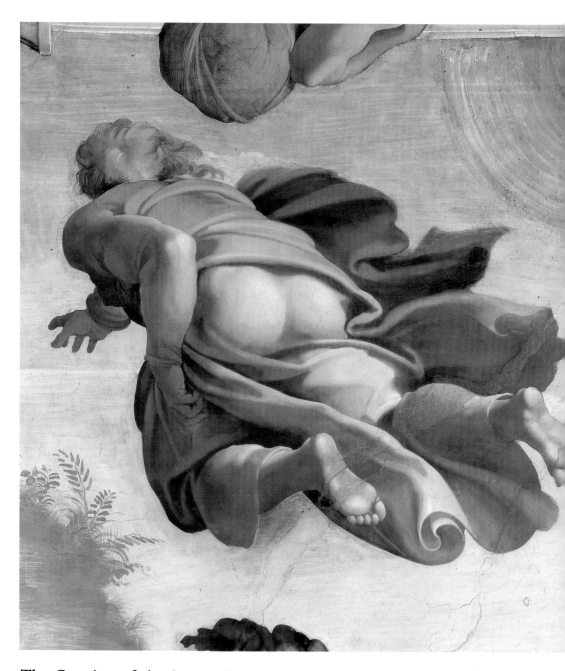

The Creation of the Sun and Moon

And God made two great lights: the greater light to rule the day, and the lesser light to rule the night; . . . (Genesis I, 16-17)

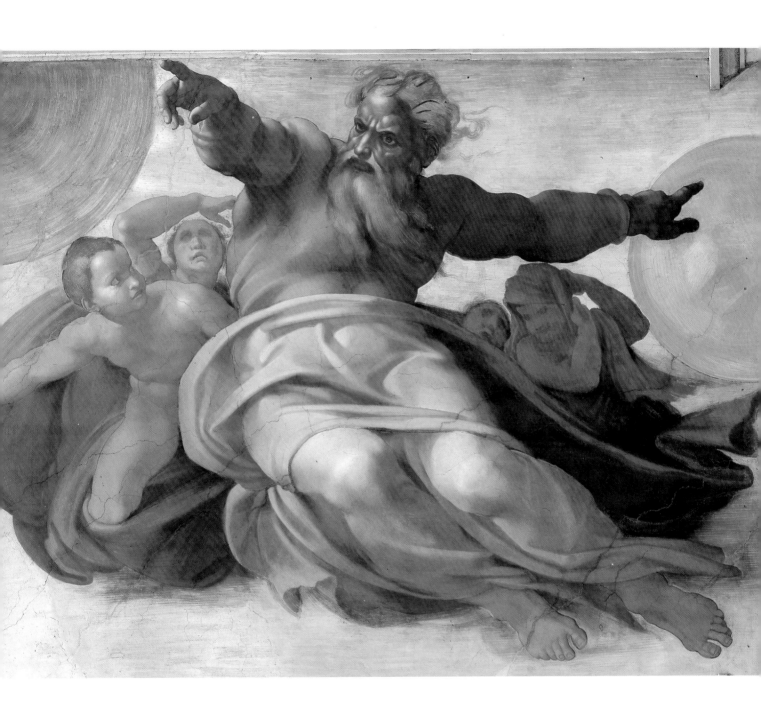

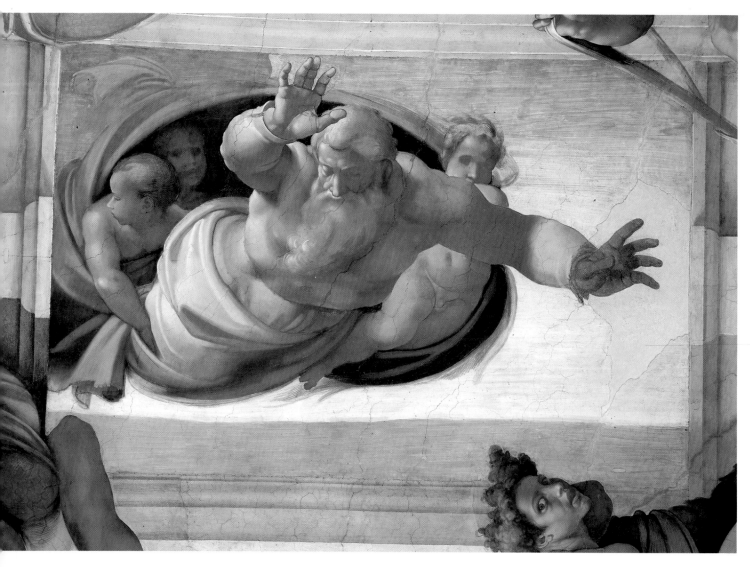

The Separation of the Sky and the Water

And God said, Let there be a firmament in the midst of the waters, and let it divide the waters from the waters. . . . (Genesis I, 6-7)

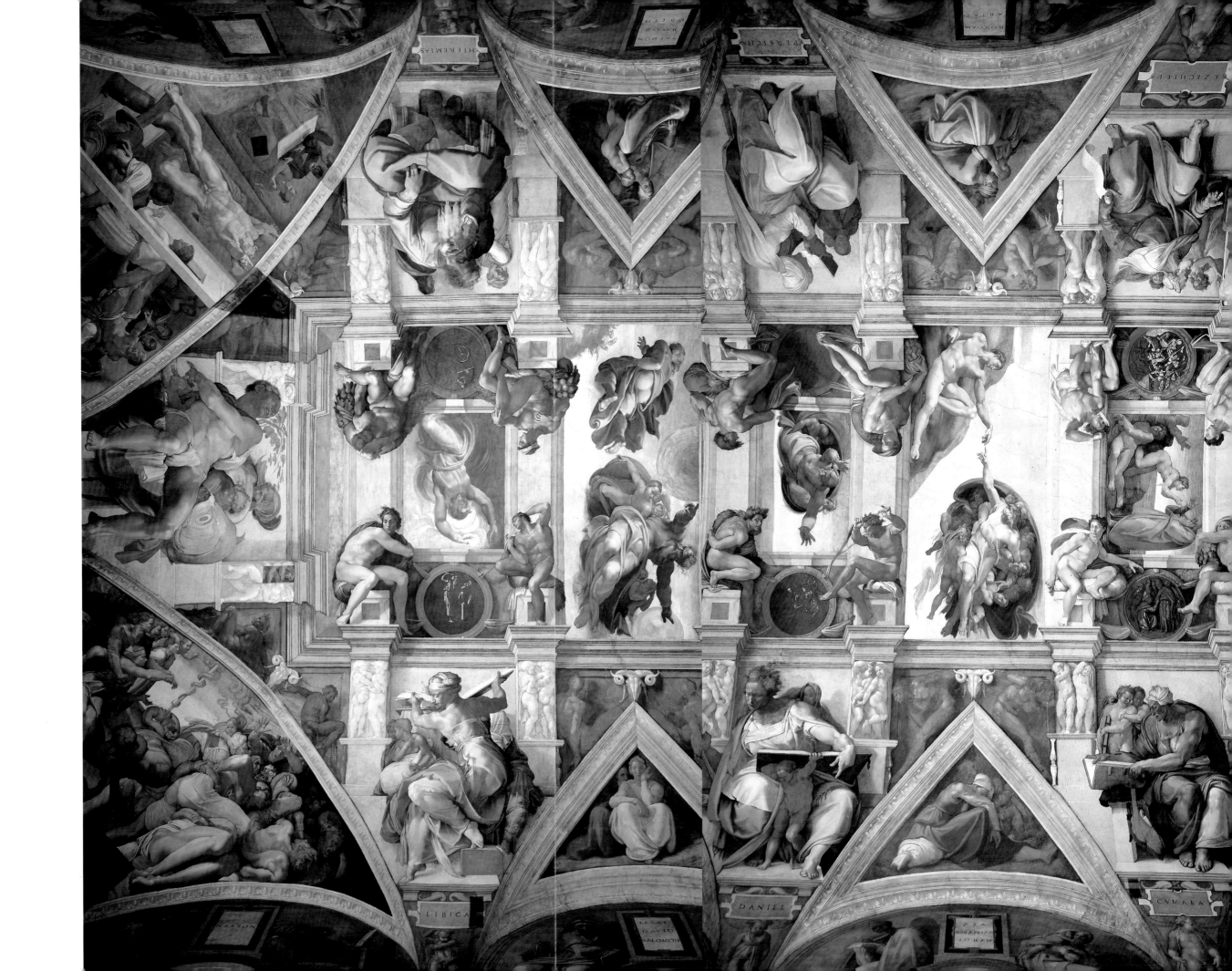

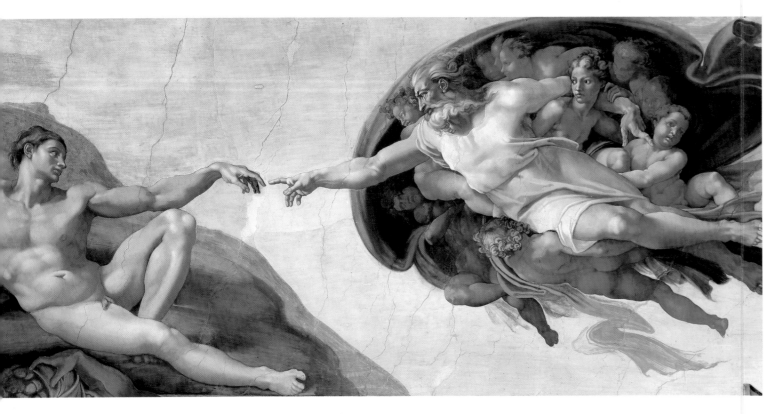

The Creation of Adam

And God said, Let us make man in our image, after our likeness; and let them have dominion over . . . all of the earth. . . . (Genesis I, 26)

The Creation of Eve

And the Lord God caused a deep sleep to fall upon Adam, and he slept; and he took one of his ribs, and closed up the flesh instead thereof; And the rib, which the Lord God had taken from man, made he a woman. . . . (Genesis II, 21-23)

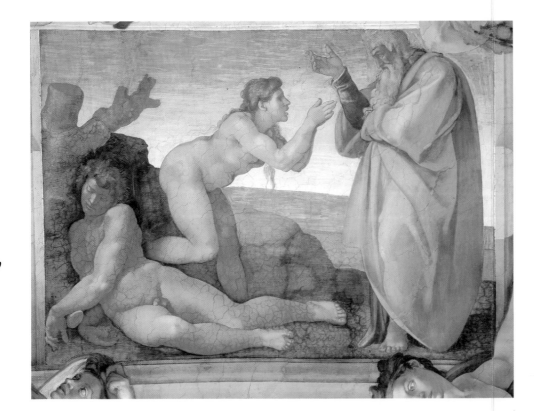

Plan of the Sistine Chapel Ceiling

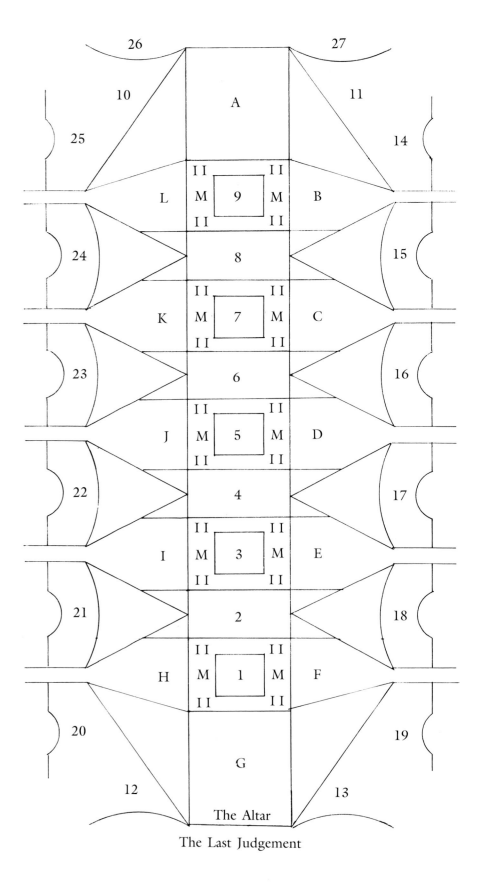

The Altar

The Last Judgement

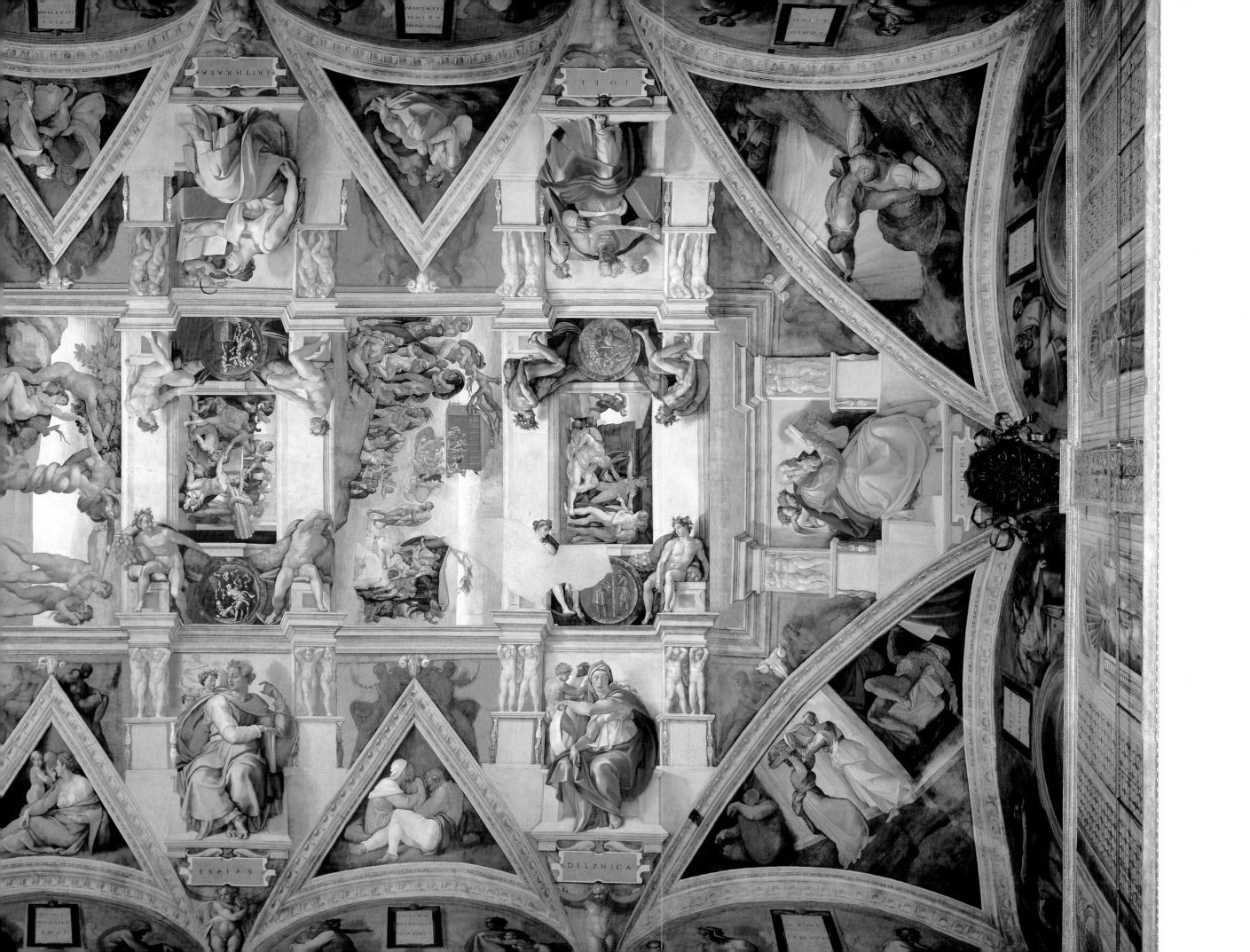

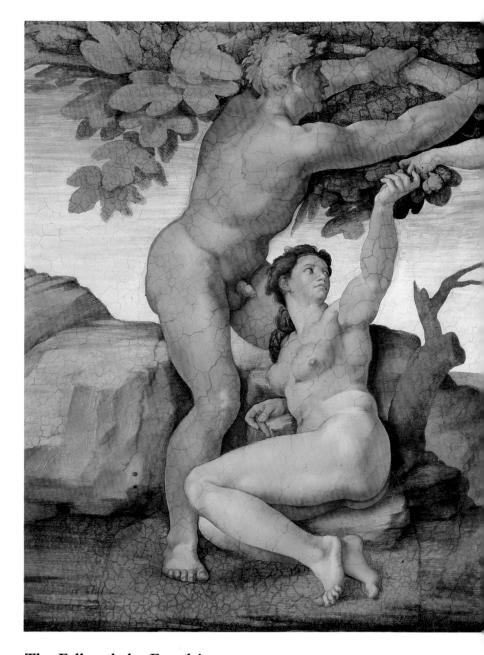

The Fall and the Expulsion

And the serpent said unto the woman, . . . ye shall be as gods, knowing good and evil.
. . . And the eyes of them both were opened, and they knew that they were naked. . . . (Genesis III, 4, 7)

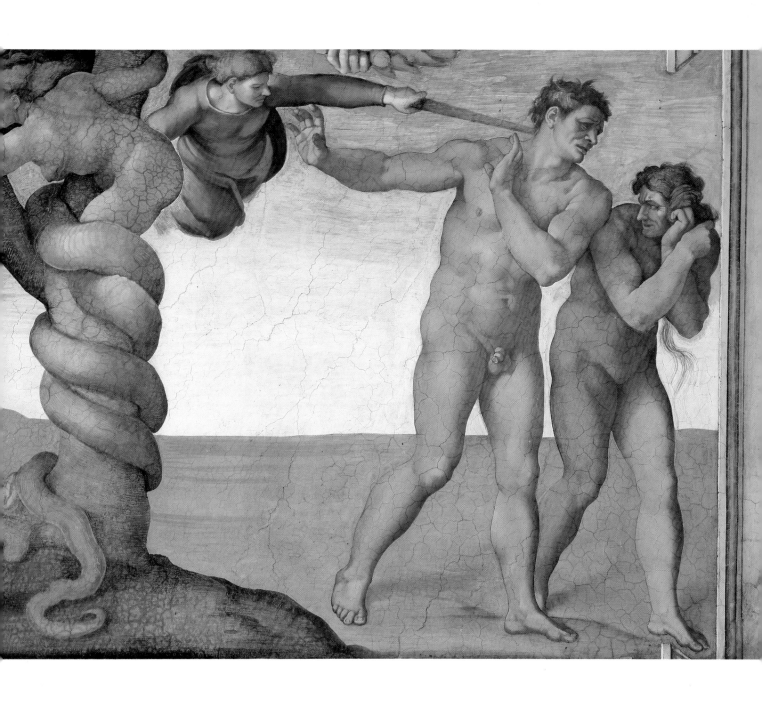

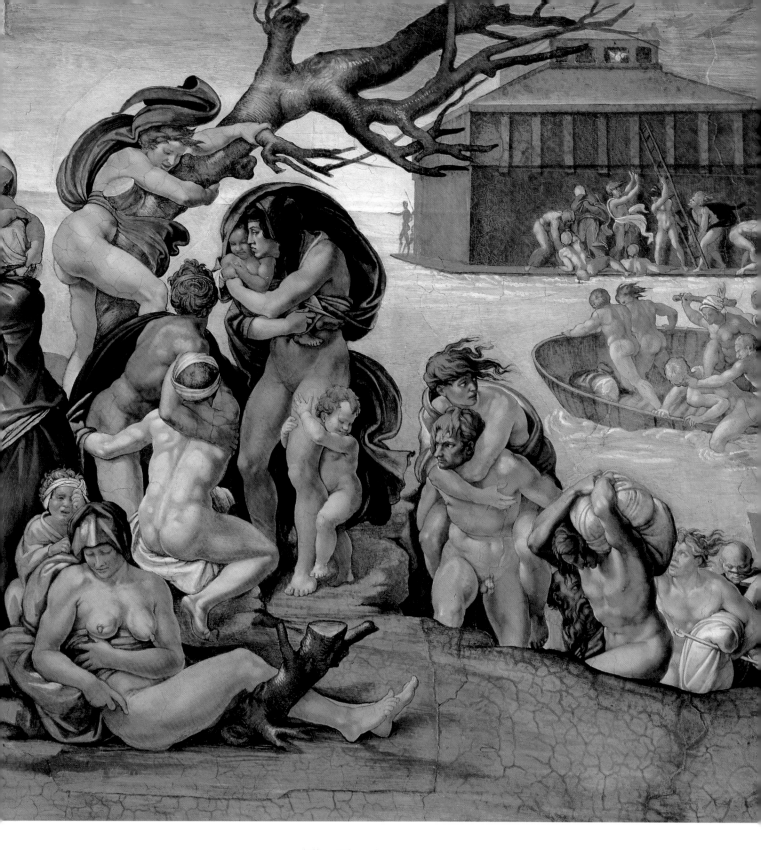

The Flood

Because it is so dramatically interesting, Michelangelo may have changed the place of this scene in the Genesis sequence, allowing it to occur after the Sacrifice.

And God said unto Noah, the end of all flesh is come before me; for the earth is filled with violence.... Make thee an ark of gopher wood; And Noah was six hundred years old when the flood of waters was upon the earth.... (Genesis VI, 13 and VII, 6)

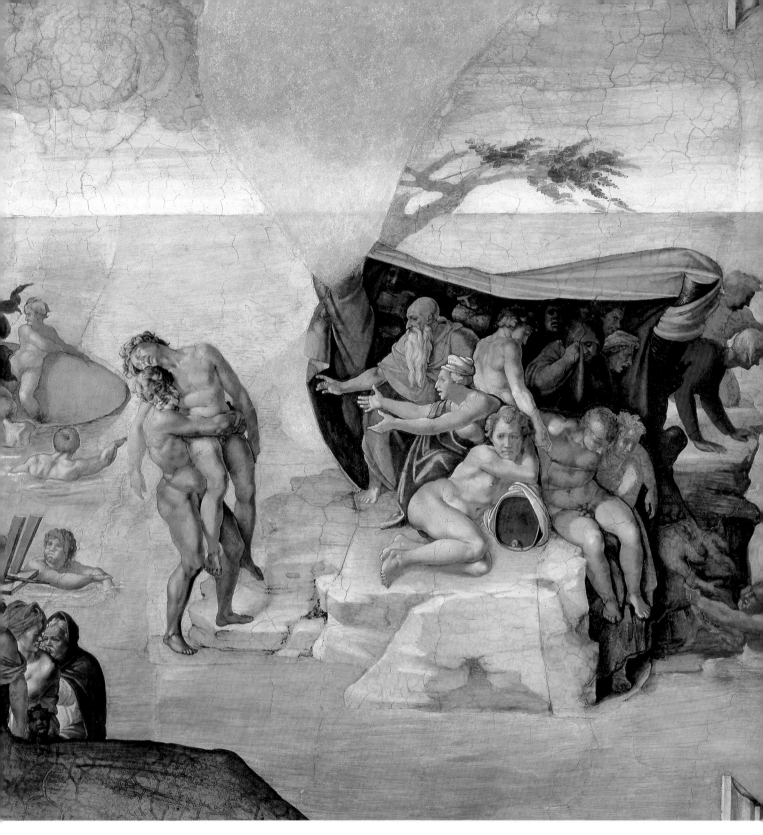

The flood follows Noah's Sacrifice *in the sequence of the ceiling.*

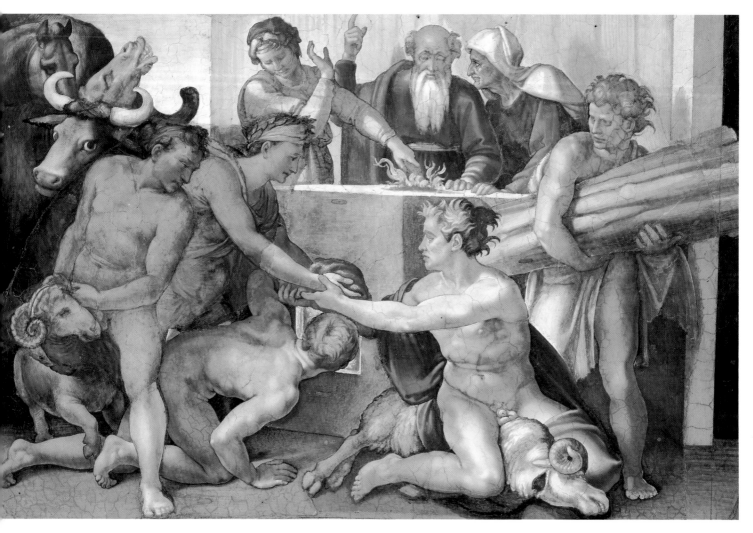

Noah's Sacrifice

This is painted out of sequential order, if indeed it is the thanksgiving of Noah for God having spared him in the Flood, and the reasons for this are unclear. Some scholars in the past have chosen to interpret it as the sacrifice of Cain and Abel, or as Abraham's sacrifice of Isaac, but this is unlikely.

And Noah builded an altar unto the Lord; and took of every clean beast, and of every clean fowl, and offered burnt offerings on the altar. (Genesis VIII, 20-21)

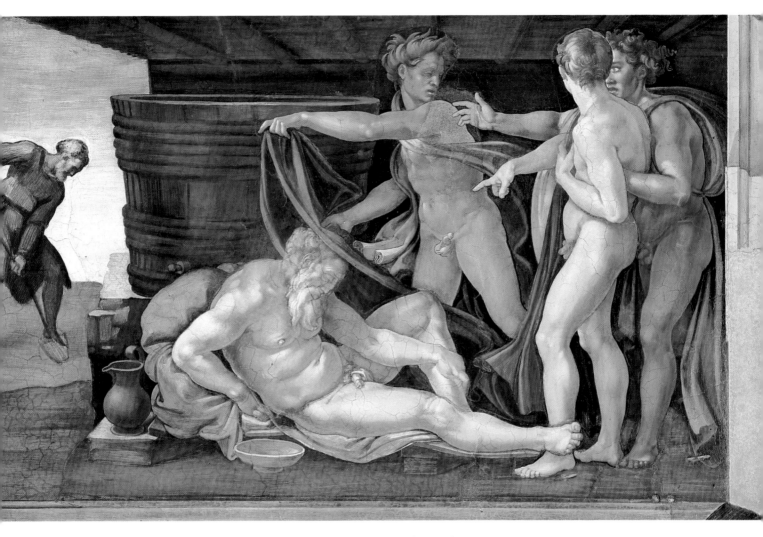

The Drunkenness of Noah

*And Noah began to be an husbandman and he planted a vineyard;
And he drank of the wine, and was drunken; and he was uncovered
within his tent. And Ham, the father of Canaan, saw the nakedness
of his father and told his two brethren without. (Genesis IX, 20-22)*

Different types of image

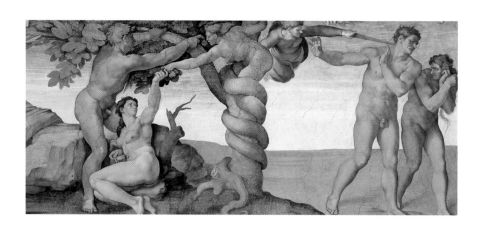

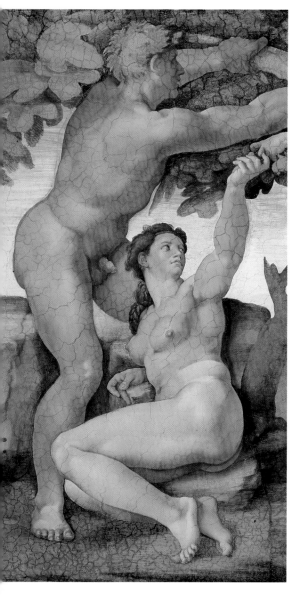

The Fall and the Expulsion

And the serpent said unto the woman, Ye shall not surely die; For God doth know that in the day ye eat thereof, then your eyes shall be opened, and ye shall be as gods, knowing good and evil.
. . . She took of the fruit thereof, and did eat, and gave also unto her husband with her; and he did eat. And the eyes of them both were opened, and they knew that they were naked.
(Genesis III, 4-7)

This panel from Genesis tells the story of Man's original sin and the expulsion of Adam and Eve in disgrace from the Garden of Eden. Very condensed in form, the panel is unified by the central device of the Tree of Knowledge, around which is wrapped the sinuous and seductive form of the serpent, a beautiful woman. Adam is plucking a fig (it is not an apple as it is often portrayed, 'apple' being a mistranslation from the Hebrew of the word 'fruit'); while his wife is shown in a delicate play of hands with the serpent. Before the Fall, Adam and Eve are youthful and handsome figures, coiled around each other in the 'serpentine' form (*la figura serpentinata*) so loved by Michelangelo, in a figure of eight. After God through His avenging angel has banished them, their faces are old and withered. They cower in shame.

This picture has proved a revelation with the present cleaning. The face of Eve on the left was in a very sorry state, showing evidence of the careless application of glue, possibly in the eighteenth century. The feathery delicacy of the painting is now once more apparent.

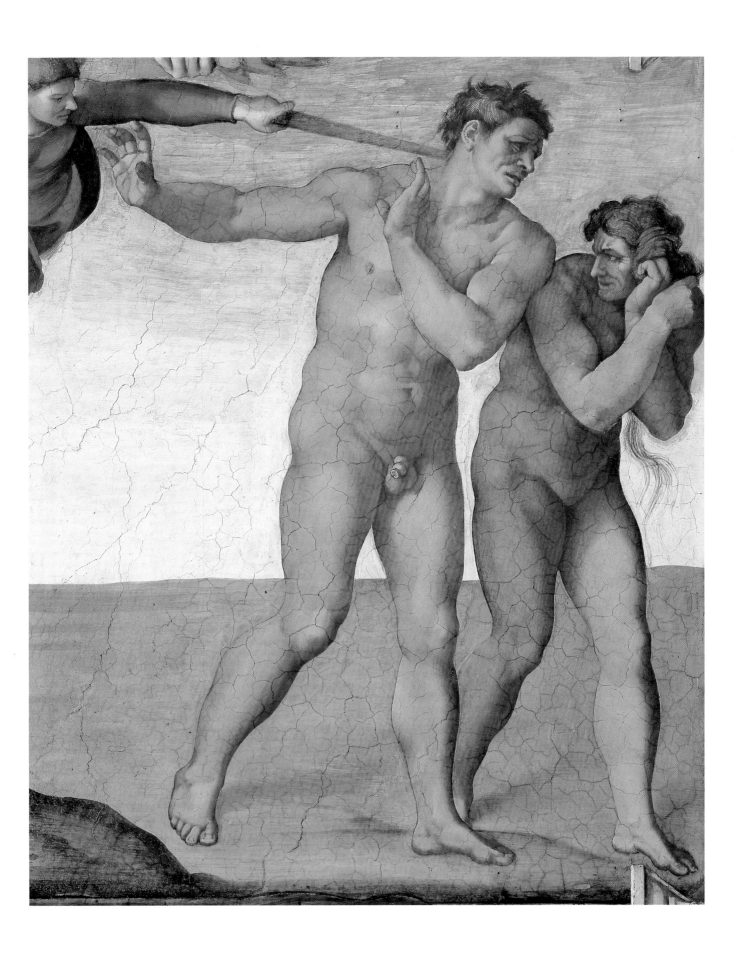

David and Goliath

And there went out a champion out of the camp of the Philistines, named Goliath, of Gath, whose height was six cubits and a span. ... David ... chose him five smooth stones out of the brook ... and his sling was in his hand, and he drew near to the Philistine. ... So David prevailed over the Philistine with a sling and with a stone, and smote the Philistine and slew him. ... (I Samuel, XVII, 4, 40, 50)

The heroic tale is depicted by Michelangelo in its last stages, as David is about to behead the giant. Michelangelo uses the device of foreshortening to convey the enormous size of Goliath. The perspective is almost excessive, as Goliath's buttocks are truly 'gigantic'. The panel makes more sense from the ground than from the scaffold where Michelangelo painted it. It shows what an amazing sense of form the artist possessed, as it would have been almost impossible to view the spandrel until the scaffolding on which he was working had been moved, when it would have been too late to make adjustments.

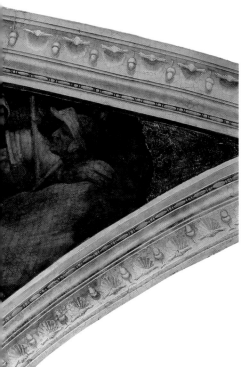

The Cumaean Sibyl

The last age, sung by the Cumaean Sibyl, is coming:
'. . . be kind to the boy being born. . . .' (Virgil, *Eclogue* IV)

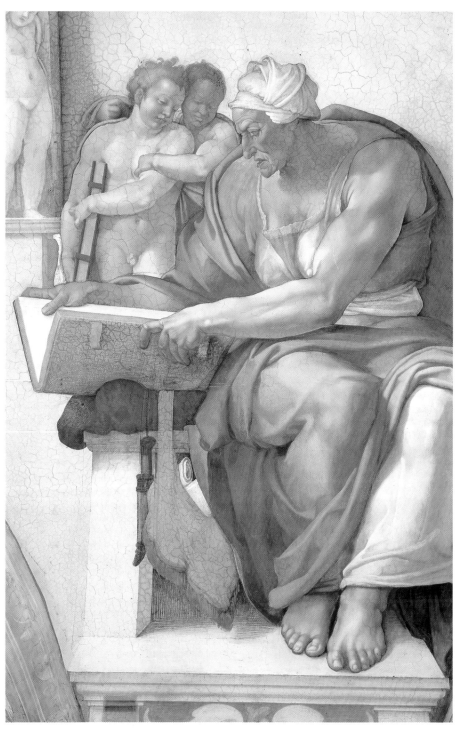

A sibyl is a figure from ancient mythology, endowed with the gift of prophecy. This figure is so strong that it is easy to believe that she would be powerful enough to predict the future. She is muscular and almost masculine. The Cumaean Sibyl is the most famous of the Sibyls, described in the Fourth *Eclogue* by the Roman poet Virgil as predicting the birth of a saviour, interpreted in Christian times as a prediction of the birth of Christ. She appears in the work of many ancient writers and seems really to have existed. She can be traced back in history many centuries before Christ. In the panel, her sternness and concentration upon her book of prophecy contrasts beautifully with the gentle whimsicality of her helpers or *genii*, who accompany most of the Prophets and Sibyls. These figures are mysterious and may be intended to embody the thoughts of the Prophets and Sibyls. They certainly provide light relief from their monumentality.

90

The Prophet Jonah

Now the Lord had prepared a great fish to swallow up Jonah. And Jonah was in the belly of the fish three days and three nights....
(Jonah I, 17)

It is difficult to believe that Michelangelo painted this figure from a vantage point less than a metre away from the wall, standing on the scaffold. It is a miracle of perspective, because the huge figure of Jonah seems to thrust violently out of the altar wall. The top half of his body, which appears to be in the process of being disgorged by the whale (or fish as it says in the Bible) is actually nearest to our eye, as the vault of the ceiling arches over our heads at that point. But Michelangelo makes it appear that the torso is farther away, and that the legs are very near to us. The opposite is actually true. This device works brilliantly from the Sistine Chapel floor where we, as viewers, are meant to be, but looks very strange and very distorted from the scaffolding, where Michelangelo stood to paint it. This is yet another example of the artist's powers of describing human form through perspective. The figure of Jonah, painted in 1511, contrasts violently with the figure of the Prophet Zecchariah, painted in 1509, being more emotional and much larger (400 x 380 cm, compared with 360 x 390 cm, or 13 x 12.5 feet compared with approximately 30 x 12 feet).

There are many theories about the gain in size of the Prophets and Sibyls from one end of the chapel to the other. Possibly the explanation is psychological, due to the artist's increase in confidence. Possibly it is because Michelangelo wants to correct the perspective of the chapel when we enter from the main entrance at the opposite end from Jonah. Because the size of the figures farther away from us is increased, they don't look quite as small as they would do without this correction.

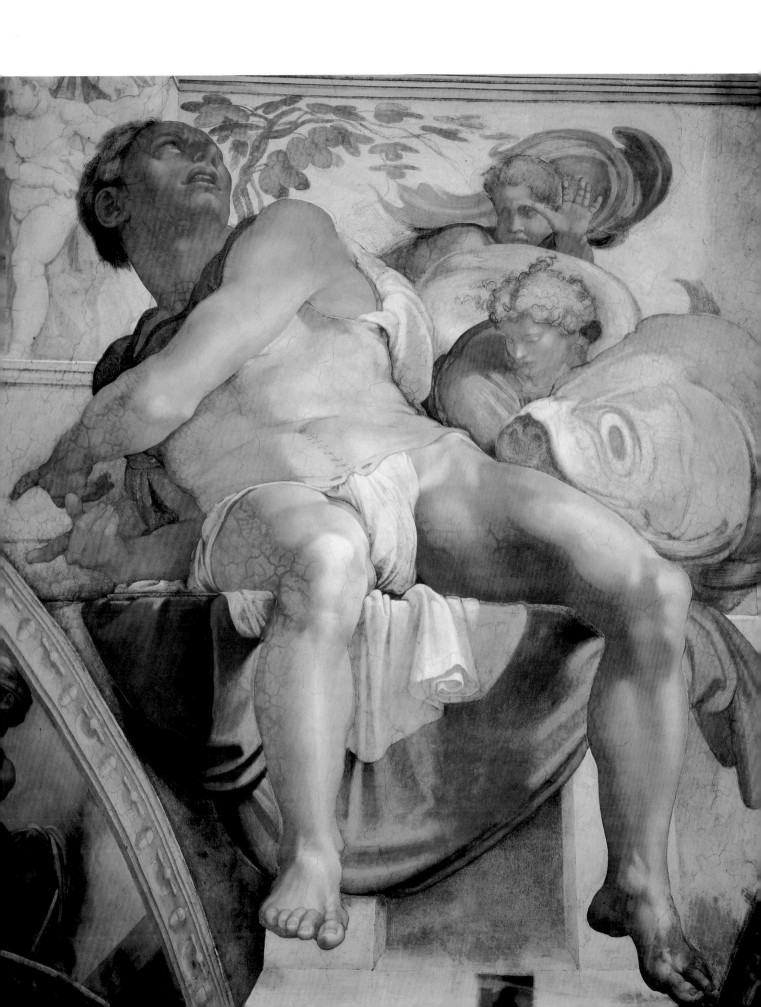

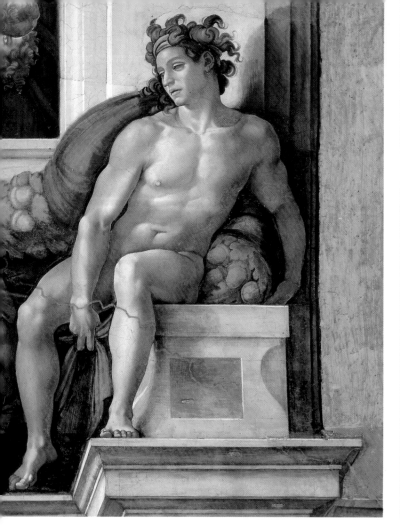
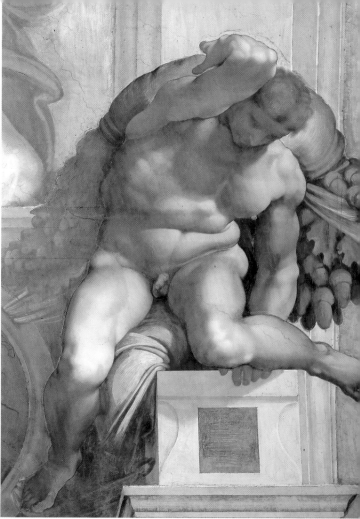

A comparison of two *ignudi*

An *ignudo* is a male nude. The meaning of Michelangelo's painted *ignudi* is open to speculation. Can they be ideal representations of human beauty, evoking Neoplatonic philosophy? Or are they simply Michelangelo doing what he does best, modelling the male figure? There are twenty of these superb figures in the design, occurring in pairs, and their most obvious function is to hold the medallions that depict scenes from the Bible. The *ignudi* are adorned with oak leaves, the symbol of the della Rovere family (*rovere* meaning oak in Italian), the family of Pope Julius.

There are great differences between the *ignudi* from the earlier stages of the ceiling, for example the one at the top right-hand corner of the *Drunkenness of Noah*, and the later ones like those from the *Division of Light from Darkness*. There are differences of size (between 150 and 180 cm or approximately 5 x 6 feet) and also of content. The earlier *ignudi* are brassier in tone and darker, showing an uneasiness with flesh colours. They are slightly stiff and posed. The later ones, such as those shown on this page, are wild and thrusting like Michelangelo's sculpture. They bear a strong similarity to the *Bound Slaves* sculpted for Julius's tomb. They use the idea of *contrapposto*, which means 'counterpoised'. This was a trademark of Michelangelo's sculpture and refers to the way the figure's weight is thrown on to one leg, while the other curves away, creating an arched, curved spine. The *ignudi* seem to want to burst their bonds and escape.

cosi l'atti suo perde chi si lega
e salvo se nessuno ma si di disciolse
(*Rime* 70)

He who is bound up and tied, cannot move
One is never truly released from his true self. . .

The lunettes of Ezekias, Manasses and Amon, and Azor and Sadoch

The book of the generation of Jesus Christ, the son of David, the son of Abraham.

Abraham begat Isaac; and Isaac begat Jacob; and Jacob begat Judas ... and Eliakim begat Azor and Azor begat Sadoch; and Sadoch begat Achim.... (Matthew, I)

The lunettes, the semicircular panels located above the windows, now number fourteen (but originally there were sixteen, including the two destroyed to make way for the *Last Judgement* on the altar wall), depicting the ancestors of Christ. They do so not in a literal sense, for it is impossible to determine which name corresponds to which figure, but in a more human sense. It seems likely that Michelangelo is trying to incorporate the idea of family life into his grand scheme. Some of the lunettes, and the small spandrels which are triangular panels above the lunettes, contain passages of extraordinary tenderness. In certain of these, in the lunette of Ezekias, Manasses and Amon for example, Michelangelo paints with greater emotion than in any other part of the chapel. Some of the lunettes are so wistful in their depiction of family love that they show real yearning. The emotion that the mother feels for her child is powerfully conveyed. Yet this was from a man who never had children of his own.

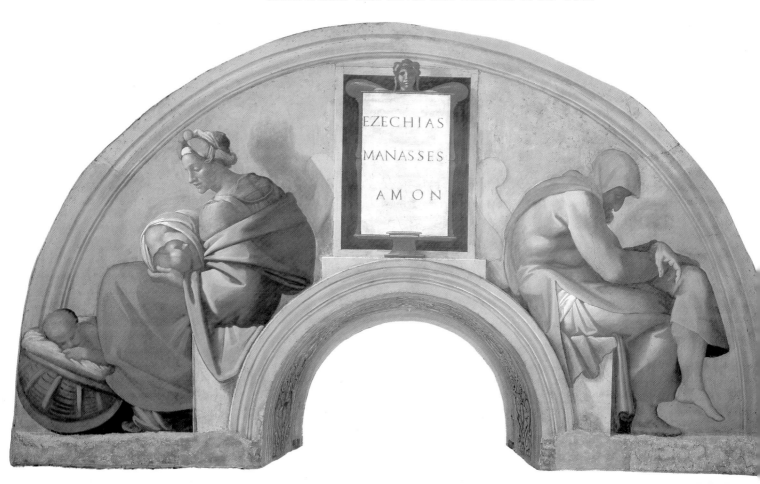

The lunettes were completed in three days of fresco work, three *giornate*. This is extremely fast. The restoration work on the ceiling project began with the lunettes and the restorers are certain that Michelangelo worked without cartoons, or preliminary sketches, and let his ideas flow directly on to the wet plaster.

The present cleaning has brought to light a probable self-portrait in the bearded man of the Azor and Sadoch lunette. Michelangelo paints himself as a shabby, elderly figure, wrapped in contemplation and far away in his own thoughts. Was Michelangelo really so prematurely aged in his late thirties? If we compare this with Raphael's portrait of him in the *School of Athens* in the Vatican *Stanze*, we see that Michelangelo has probably painted his exhausted state of mind rather than his actual physical appearance.

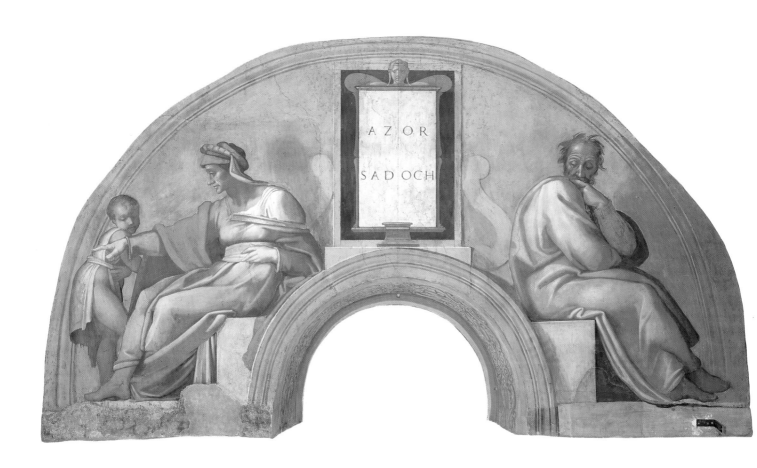

6 The Technique of Fresco Painting

Although the effect of the ceiling is revolutionary, the painting technique has a long history. The form of painting used by Michelangelo on the Sistine Chapel ceiling is called *fresco* painting. Cennino Cennini, in his classic book of 1390, *Il Libro dell' Arte*, called it 'the sweetest and most attractive way of working there is'. Fresco means 'fresh' in Italian, and refers to the fact that the wall which receives the painting must be freshly plastered. The technique ensures that the painting will be long-lasting and strong, although the restoration of the Sistine Chapel ceiling has revealed how candle-soot, water, grime and human interference can damage it. By its very nature, fresco painting 'becomes' the wall in a fascinating chemical process, which is explained later in this chapter. Vasari, biographer of many artists and an early art expert, asserts:

(Fresco) resists both atmosphere and water and will always withstand any kind of knock. . . . May those who want to paint on a wall, work courageously in fresco and let them not retouch *a secco*, because besides being cowardly, it shortens the life of a painting.

The need for courage will become clear later.

Fresco painting is an art that is almost lost to the twentieth century, but it had been known and used since ancient times. We are used to squeezing paint like toothpaste out of tubes and going into art shops to buy ready-made paper and canvases. The modern painter has no idea of the chemistry of his or her material. The Renaissance painter was much more of a craftsman. He was trained in all branches of science pertaining to art, from mathematics (used in perspective drawing) to chemistry (how the paint is made). He knew how to grind the materials mined from the earth and produce colours ranging from the richest yellows (such as Mars yellow made from iron-oxide hydrates and the ochres) to the richest reds (ochres and natural iron oxides). He knew how a wall must be prepared in order to paint upon it and was familiar with the subtleties of masonry and of rendering and plastering the surface, ready for the paint. The Renaissance painter was a true humanist in that he was engaged in all the different facets of human experience, whether art or science, philosophy or religion.

Michelangelo is one of the great masters of the fresco technique. Ghirlandaio had trained him well. Though he was dogged by technical problems at the beginning of his painting of the Sistine Chapel ceiling, especially in the *Flood* where the fresco was attacked by mould, due, according to Vasari, to overwetting of the wall, he achieved his marvellous results through expert devotion to the material and stubborn commitment. At times he worked practically alone, assisted only by the mason who prepared the wall and the grinder of the paints. For four long years he stood precariously and painfully on a scaffold, craning his neck upwards for hour upon hour. He became so fixed in this terrible position, on or off the scaffold, that he could only read if he held the book over his head in the same position that he used to paint the ceiling.

Unlike other fresco painters, Michelangelo was not very happy employing assistants, *garzoni*, to help him with the less important details, but it is clear that he did have some help. The painting of the medallions shows this tangibly. As they have become more clearly revealed by the cleaning, it is obvious that they are fairly complex in the first, eastern half of the ceiling, painted before 1511, and very sketchy after this date. The change in style relates to the reduction in the number of assistants Michelangelo used. The restoration work has also revealed that at least six people worked at different times on the fictive architecture of the ceiling in the cornices – the restorers have learned to recognize Michelangelo's own brushmark, just as if it were his handwriting.

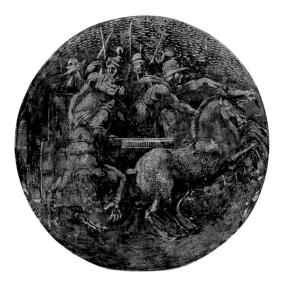

Medallion from the eastern end of the ceiling, probably painted before 1511.

Generally Michelangelo found it hard to get on with people. Vasari talks of Granaccio, Giulian Bugiardini, Iacopo di Sandro, Indaco the Elder, Agnolo di Donnino and Aristotile helping Michelangelo in the early stages of work on the ceiling. Vasari also recounts how Michelangelo locked them out of the chapel in a fit of temper. He was a perfectionist and his exacting standards did not permit a stable relationship with apprentices and assistants, who could never live up to those standards. But when in later years he boasted to his biographers that he worked alone on the ceiling for most of the time, he was either deliberately forgetting the difficult times, or he was ensuring that history would view the Sistine Chapel ceiling as the achievement of only one man. Of course the achievement is Michelangelo's, but it is impossible not to be curious about the contribution of the *garzoni*.

To begin a fresco, the painter must first prepare his paint. He – or usually his assistant – grinds the earth colour derived from minerals in a mortar and pestle with purified water, making up a paste of a smooth consistency like cream. He then awaits the call from his plasterer that the wall is ready. Usually the plasterer has worked all night preparing the *intonaco*, which is the smooth, flat, final layer of plaster that will hold the painting. The *intonaco* is

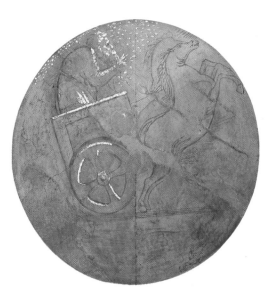

Medallion from the western end, painted later.

often the fourth or fifth layer, and is placed over a rougher skin of plaster called the *arriccio*. The plasterer uses a mixture of limestone which has been ground very fine and cleaned (or 'slaked') over months; *pozzolana* (ground volcanic powder); and water. Sometimes sand or marble dust and even animal hair is added to the mixture. All these ingredients are mixed into a plaster that has the consistency of thick mud and dries fairly quickly.

The plasterer is an expert at removing all the bumps and ridges in the wall with his trowel. Despite this expertise, it is amazing how bumpy the surface of the Sistine Chapel ceiling is when viewed very closely from the scaffolding. It looks like a rippling sea. This is probably the fault of the original builders of the chapel in the fifteenth century, but must certainly have caused Michelangelo some problems.

The artist must paint on the plaster while it is still wet for the chemical process to work. The wall must not be too wet, however, or the paint will drip. It is clearly necessary to have skill, patience and expertise.

The paint is applied on to the wet plaster in fairly small areas. Partly because the lime in the plaster can develop mould or *efflorescence*, the areas must be confined to what the painter can manage in a day, a *giornata*, which literally means a day's work. Looked at very carefully, the edges of each day's work can be seen in Michelangelo's painting. The edges of each new area of plaster are slightly raised. Also, when he has used a *cartoon*, his incision into the wet plaster is very visible. A cartoon is a large preparatory drawing on paper which is held against the wall, and lightly pasted to it. The lines of the drawing are transferred to the wall beneath in two ways. Either the lines are 'pounced', when small holes are made along the line and charcoal dust is blown through on to the wall; or the lines are actually drawn through the paper with a sharp point. Few cartoons for fresco survive, as they end up in tatters.

All this detail brings Michelangelo very close to us and we can imagine his sense of urgency and excitement as he raced against the clock to complete the day's section. The fresco painter has

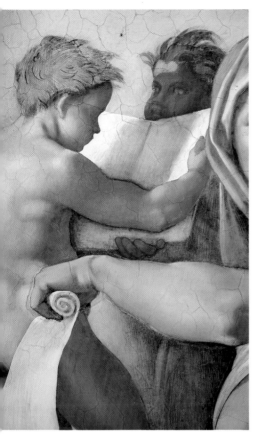

Detail from the Delphic Sibyl. The line of her raised arm clearly illustrates the scar-like ridge that defines a giornata.

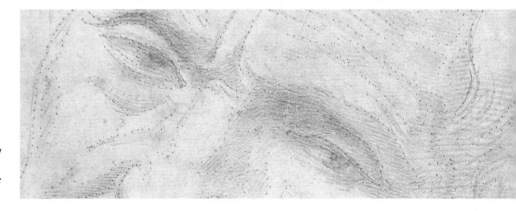

Detail of the drawing of Michelangelo by Daniele da Volterra, showing the prick marks used to transfer the drawing to the wall for fresco painting.

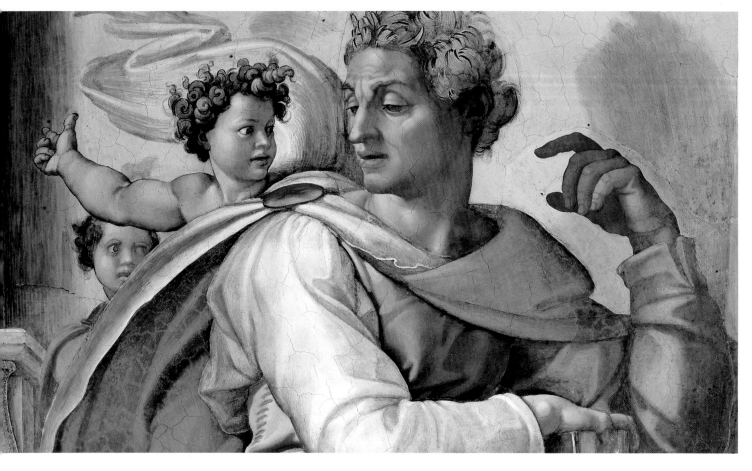

Detail of the Prophet Isaiah, showing rapid brush strokes.

only between eight and a maximum of twelve hours before the plaster is too dry for the chemical fusion of paint and plaster to work. Michelangelo worked with extraordinary rapidity, as can be seen from the large areas of the *giornate*. The *giornate* of the lunettes (the semi-circular panels above the windows) are huge, and it is very clear that he did not use cartoons at all in these, preferring to draw with a brush dipped in dark-brown pigment directly on to the *intonaco*. Michelangelo's fresco technique allowed for a little extra time, since he used the paint thinly, placing a wash of one diluted colour over another, to create a glowing transparency rare in fresco. In Italian, these washes or glazes are called *velature*, meaning veils. His teacher Ghirlandaio used this technique in Florence, but Michelangelo takes it much further in Rome. Raphael, working at the same time, in the same city and in the same medium, used paint very differently. The paintings of the papal apartments, the *Stanze*, are less transparent and give less of a sense of solidity and mass. But even Michelangelo was forced by the limits of time to finish his painting while the plaster was still fairly wet, or it would never have lasted.

Michelangelo was very faithful to the spirit of fresco, as advocated by Vasari, and treated each day's work as the finished product. If, as was sometimes the case, he was displeased with a

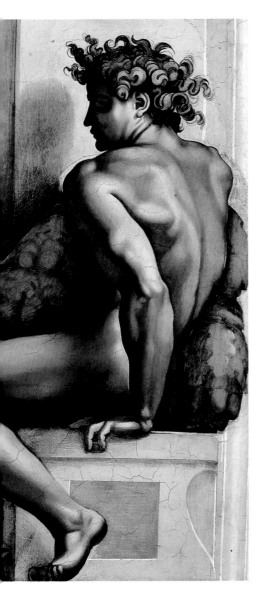

Detail of ignudo.

piece of work, he could scrape off the offending section and have his plasterer remove the *intonaco* altogether. This is called a *pentimento*, which means a 'repentance'. Alternatively, the *intonaco* could be lightly scraped off, and a new painting surface of fresh lime be painted on thinly with a brush. This is known as *mezzo* (half) *fresco*. There are many *pentimenti* in the ceiling.

By its very nature, fresco cannot be erased like paint on a canvas or paper; but Michelangelo hardly used the '*a secco*' technique of which, as has been shown, Vasari disapproved. This technique involves putting dry, *secco*, paint on top of an already dried piece of fresco painting. Where it does occur on the Sistine Chapel ceiling, it has raised problems for the current restoration and cleaning project, because the restorers have to be sure that it is not the *a secco* painting by Michelangelo that is removed on their sponges as they clean different parts of the ceiling with the solvent A.B. 57. When *a secco* work is determined to be by Michelangelo, such as the bent arm of the *ignudo* to the right of the Prophet Joel, it is fixed with Paraloid B 72, a gel that isolates the water from the soluble *a secco* parts. Sadly for the Vatican restorers, other people have worked *a secco* on the ceiling, which makes their job very difficult. For of course, unlike true fresco, *secco* painting is neither waterproof nor permanent, since there is no chemical bonding. In removing other people's additions, they risk destroying Michelangelo's own work.

The glory of real fresco technique, *buon fresco*, is that the painter has to commit himself while the plaster is still wet and this is why Vasari calls *a secco* painting 'cowardly'.

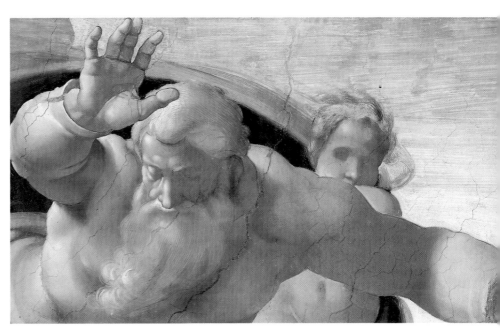

Detail from the Separation of the Sky and the Water *showing delicate* chiaroscuro *and rapid brushwork in the background*.

The basic chemistry of the process is as follows:

Calcium hydroxide, which is created by the combination of the

Colour	+ Plaster (slaked lime)	+ Water (purified)	+ Carbon dioxide (from the air)	becomes the fresco layer
Pigment	+ $Ca(OH)_2$ calcium hydroxide	+ H_2O	+ CO_2	> $CaCO_3$ + pigment = calcium carbonate

lime in the plaster and the water in the paint, rises to the surface of the wall as it dries, and reacts with the **carbon dioxide** in the air to create a crust of **calcium carbonate** which holds the paint permanently. Fresco painters call this carbonization.

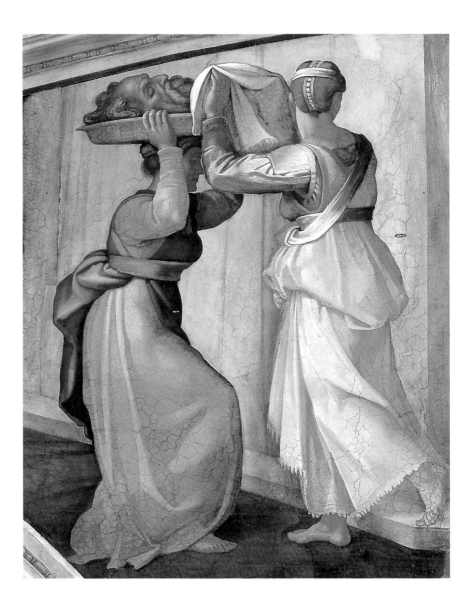

Detail from the spandrel of Judith and Holofernes where transparent layers of colour are used on the draperies.

Detail from the lunette depicting Asa, with glowing washes of colour.

Detail from the panel of the Fall and the Expulsion, *showing the layers of colours on the serpent.*

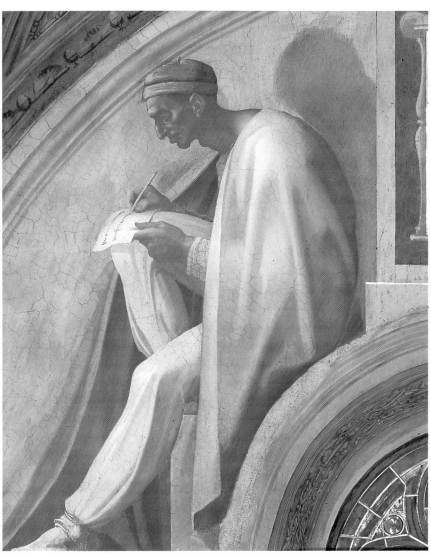

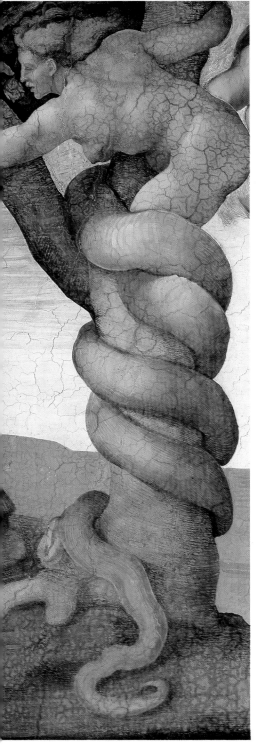

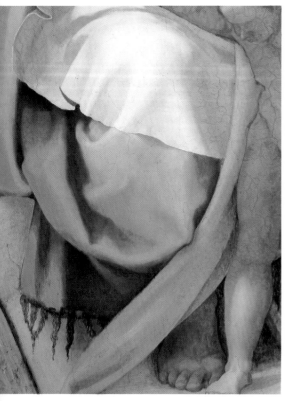

Detail of the Prophet Daniel's knee.

A great variety of tones was achieved by Michelangelo within a limited range of colours, by using them transparently, placing one veil of colour over another. Sometimes this was done by cross-hatching the painting of countless tiny lines with a fine brush. Sometimes he used a larger brush, sweeping colour over colour, when the lower colour was almost, but not completely, dry. Thus a veil of luscious yellow placed over white and *terre verte* underneath, in the Prophet Daniel's knee, creates the optical illusion that there is orange in Daniel's skirt when there is none. The colour seems to fizz with energy. As a painter myself, I am lost in admiration at his magnificent understanding of the 'cookery' skills in painting.

Michelangelo understood that in fresco painting only the purest earth colours will join in the chemical process successfully. He is revealed as an exuberant colourist now the centuries of grime and abuse have been carefully wiped away by the restoration team.

It is not necessary to understand the chemistry in order to grasp why fresco painting is unique in its ability to outlast any other medium of painting. Oil paint cracks over time, and wood panels and canvases warp. Watercolour on paper fades and is easily damaged by sunlight. Fresco lasts as long as the wall itself, though it is as vulnerable to dirt as any other medium. We are indebted to the restorers who have cleaned Michelangelo's ceiling. The next chapter will show how the problems of centuries of dirt, grime, soot, decayed varnish, glue, and other people's mistakes, have been addressed. It is a tribute to the technique of fresco painting that it has proved to be resistant even to such pernicious damage.

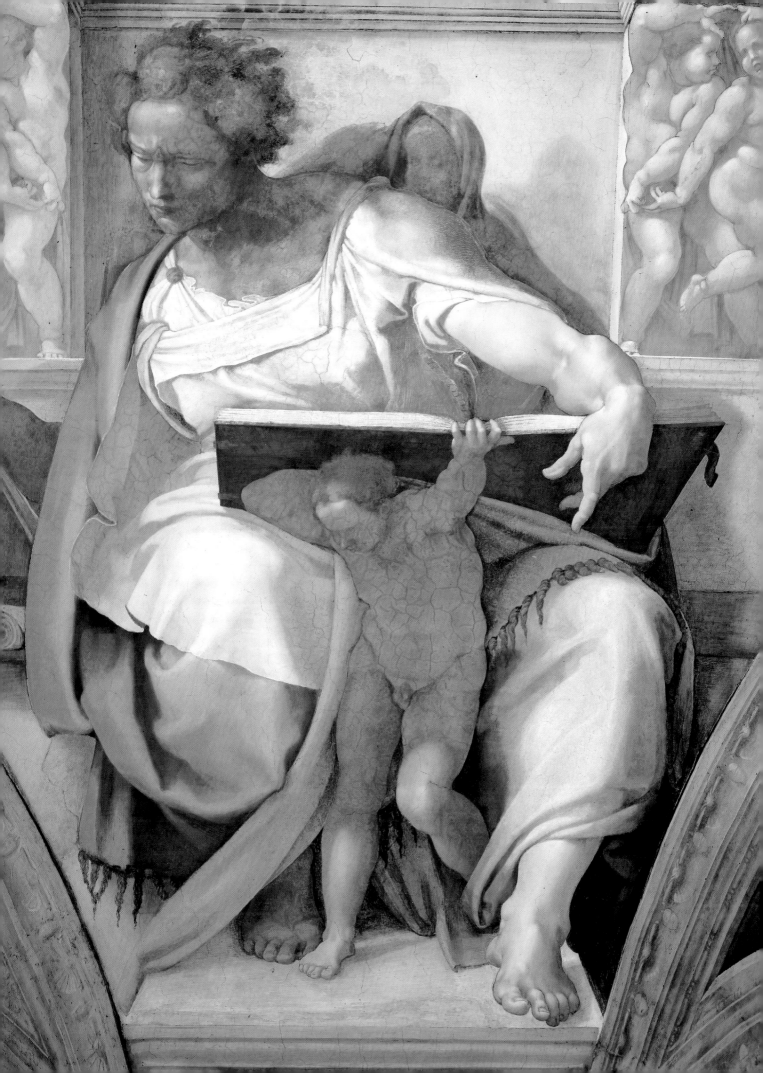

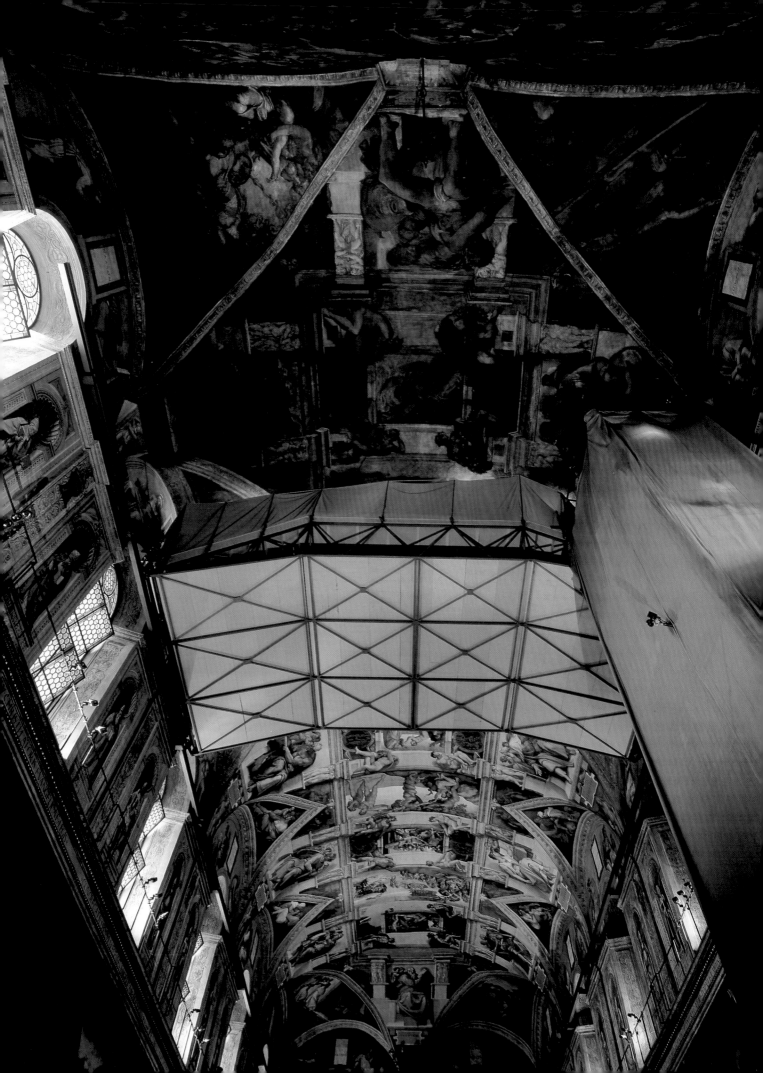

7 Revealing the Sistine Chapel Ceiling

In 1975, to celebrate the five-hundredth anniversary of the birth of Michelangelo, the Vatican set to work on the long-overdue restoration of the roof space above the Sistine Chapel. Rain had been leaking into the ceiling for centuries, and various attempts at restoration are recorded, as follows.

1547   In Michelangelo's lifetime, Paolo Giovio told Vasari, Michelangelo's biographer, about the ever-widening cracks appearing in the painting. He also commented on the presence of whitish spots, the result of salt deposits in the rainwater, saying that parts of the ceiling appeared to be 'in a poor condition'.

1565–66   About two years after Michelangelo's death, the Modenese restorer Domenico Carnevale began work on restoration of the ceiling, filling in cracks and repainting damaged figures in *Noah's Sacrifice*. Matteo da Lecce and Hendrick van der Broeck were brought in to work on repairing damaged frescoes on the wall opposite the *Last Judgement*, caused by subsidence of the whole building from 1504 to 1565.

1625   The next major cleaning operation: Pope Urban VIII commissioned the resident restorer and gilder Lagi, who was a well-known Florentine painter, who first dusted the ceiling with a linen cloth and then lifted the dust with slices of bread, sometimes 'moistened a little'.

1710-12   Annibale Mazzuoli and two assistants worked on the ceiling, using sponges dipped in Greek wine, which acted as a temporary revivifier of what must have already appeared to be fading colours. (The Sistine Chapel will certainly have smelled like a cheap hostelry with all those sour fumes wafting down from the ceiling!) This is the likely period of the most damaging intervention on Michelangelo's ceiling –

View of the ceiling of the Sistine Chapel showing the mobile platform on which the restorers worked, and the access lift on the right. The cleaned portion of the ceiling is clearly visible in the bottom half of this photograph.

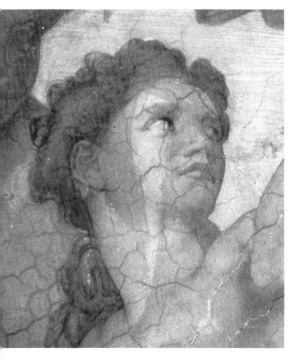

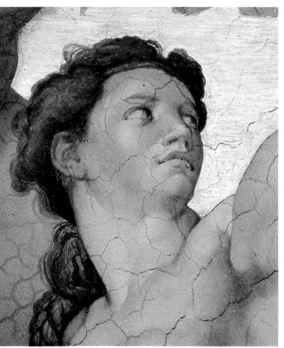

The head of Eve, from the panel depicting the Fall and the Expulsion, *showing the haphazard application of a coat of animal glue, before and after cleaning.*

possibly done by Mazzuoli himself. Yet the restorer cannot have foreseen the dire consequences of his work. A thick layer of animal glue was painted haphazardly over the whole ceiling. It was carelessly applied, missing out certain areas altogether, such as part of Eve's face. To those who maintain that Michelangelo himself was responsible for this, it can only be said that such a perfectionist would never have been so careless. This was probably neither the first nor the last occasion when a restorer relied on this ultimately naive method of 'fixing' Michelangelo's colours, so we must not be too hard on him, whoever he was. There is evidence of other applications of unidentified remedies to the ailing ceiling.

1762 Other small interventions on the vault were made, probably by a man called Pozzi – crude 'touch-ups' with crayons, oil paint and tempera. These were attempts to give definition to the figures, growing fainter as they retreated into the penumbra of dirt. In 1787 the great German writer Goethe reports regretfully that the frescoes are 'darkened'.

1797 An explosion occurred in the nearby Castel Sant'Angelo, causing a large section of the *Flood* to come crashing to the floor, and also the loss of an *ignudo*, above the *Flood*. The missing patch of the *Flood* was plastered over and an attempt made to paint it. The patch can still be seen.

1825 Camuccini cleaned parts of the ceiling and the *Last Judgement*.

1904 Seitz consolidated the vault, having attempted to clean the paintings, but then abandoning the tests for fear of damage to Michelangelo's work. Cingolani and Cecconi-Principi also worked in the chapel.

1920-40 Biagetti did further work on the vault in the 1920s and 1930s. He carried out a thorough consolidation of the vault.

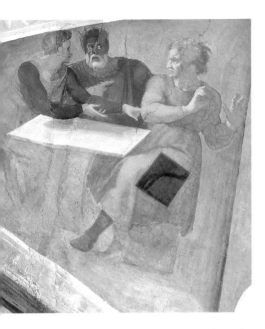

A detail from the spandrel of the Punishment of Haman. *The dark square shows the condition before cleaning.*

When the present campaign of work was begun in 1980, under the stewardship of Gianluigi Colalucci, head of the Conservation Laboratory of the Vatican Museum, the ceiling was in a terrible state. Tests revealed to no one's surprise that the ceiling was covered in dust, fatty particles and soot. This came from the burning of candles and oil lamps in the papal chapel and from Roman traffic and air pollution. The dirt had become attached to the layer of dense animal glue applied over the frescoes. The dust and soot were worrying enough, but the real problem was perceived to be that the colour from Michelangelo's frescoes was pulling away from the wall, caused by the contraction of the glue due to variations in temperature.

The first steps in the cleaning project were taken slowly and carefully. The international community of scholars, artists and restorers was consulted and opinions were evaluated. Some people felt strongly that the Sistine Chapel was too important a work to use as a guinea pig for revolutionary new cleaning methods. There was public outcry, particularly in the United States. Other experts were convinced of the necessity to act. The grime of centuries and the foolish pieces of retouching would be finally removed once and for all in this programme and the ceiling's structure carefully consolidated. The art world split into two camps. There were those who were convinced of the ethical and technical merits of the project and those who were in despair. The Sistine Chapel has always elicited such extremes of emotion.

The Vatican authorities were very open about the cleaning project. Their team took up a public position at the forefront of scientific enterprise, using every new piece of technology available, much of it donated by private institutions. The community of scholars was invited to inspect work in progress and to comment. But the project became the focus of antagonism and hostility, attitudes which still persist in some quarters.

Michelangelo would have been highly amused by it all and possibly not a little put out. His personal vision expressed in paint was examined under every conceivable light, from normal quartz to ultraviolet, fluorescent, infrared and sodium chromatic rays. Microscopic samples of pigment were taken downstairs to the lab and examined under infrared spectrometry and liquid chromatography. Minute particles were analysed with an atomic absorption spectrophotometer. I myself had the intense pleasure of examining stratigraphic sections of Michelangelo's work in the lab. Through a powerful microscope I could clearly see a layer of glue over a layer of pigment over a layer of lime in a tiny speck of paint. It seemed a million miles away from the spirit of art and of Michelangelo. Yet it also brought him closer to me, as his marks came sharply into focus under the microscope.

Scientific rigour has characterised the whole of the Sistine

Chapel cleaning programme. The analysis I have outlined has never faltered in its attention to detail. Every step along the way has been meticulously documented. It was very odd indeed to see a computer, furnished with the most sophisticated and specialised software, sitting next to shabby old buckets on the high-technology scaffolding that was used to clean the ceiling (set into the same holes used by Michelangelo). Yet, upon my request to see the state of conservation of a certain part of the ceiling, the information was yielded up instantly on the computer screen.

So why, if everything is so scientifically rigorous, has there been so much fuss about the project? The answer is complex, but basically comes down to two questions. Does the ceiling look now as it did when Michelangelo painted it? How can we be sure?

The argument that the cleaning has removed Michelangelo's final layer of paint is based on an interpretation of a small remark by Ascanio Condivi, referring to the fact that Michelangelo wanted to put *l'ultima mano* on the frescoes before declaring them finished. This has been interpreted by certain scholars as meaning a final coat of varnish, used by Michelangelo to 'unify' the overall effect of the ceiling. But the words literally mean 'the last hand', more accurately translated as 'final touches'. Condivi recounts that Michelangelo never did apply *l'ultima mano*, being in a great rush to finish the ceiling. He wanted to disassemble the scaffolding and get home to see his family in Florence. His statement, also quoted by Condivi, '*e così rimasta*' ('and so it stayed the way it was') implies very strongly that Michelangelo actually did nothing to the ceiling when it was finished in *buon fresco*.

Michelangelo was probably referring to the small sections of *a secco* painting that were needed to add gold leaf to the medallions. The issue of *a secco* painting is contentious, hinging on the question of what was, or was not, Michelangelo's work. There are those scholars who believe that Michelangelo relied heavily on this form of adjustment. According to the team of restorers, however, though there is some *a secco* work by him in the first part of the ceiling, up to the beginning of 1511, the amount is comparatively small. They believe they can recognize his own work and that there is very little in the second half.

Another source of anger for the 'against' brigade, who have at various times used terms such as 'artistic Chernobyl' to describe the restoration, to which they refer scathingly as 'industrial', is the substance used to clean the ceiling. The cleaning agent is A.B. 57 and is a weak solution of sodium bicarbonate and ammonium bicarbonate which is suspended in a gelatin called carboxymethyl-cellulose. The gell is inactive and only serves to keep the solution on the fresco. The solution is applied to small areas in three-minute applications. Each application is removed with distilled

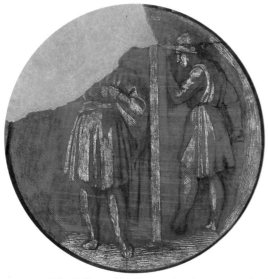

A medallion with Michelangelo's 'final touches' of gold.

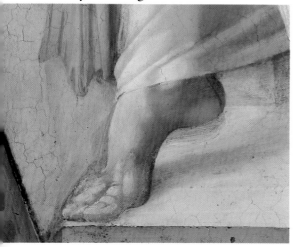

The Libyan Sibyl's foot has been reworked into a more graceful position, a secco. *The team of restorers consider this work to be by Michelangelo.*

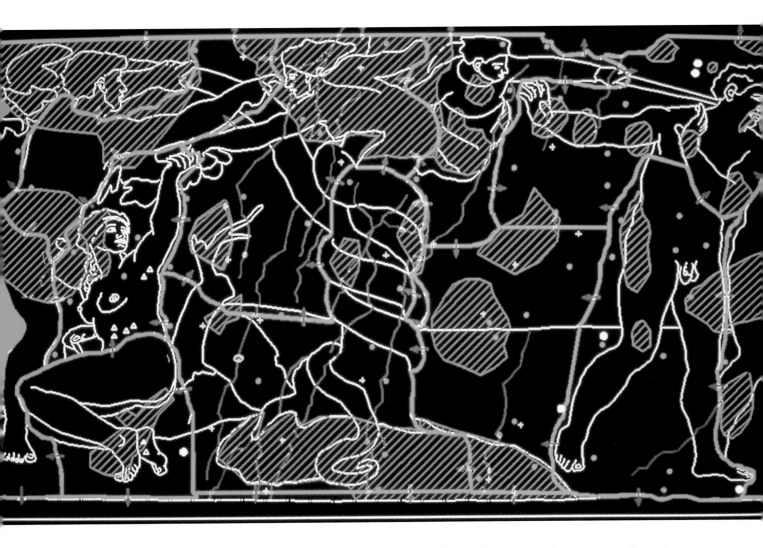

A *'bit map' of the* Fall and the Expulsion: *a computer diagram of the condition of this panel.*

water and the area is allowed to rest for twenty-four hours between applications. There are usually three applications. The water removed is then chemically analysed to determine whether any of Michelangelo's paint is coming off in the process. The restorers are able to take a sort of time 'fingerprint' of Michelangelo's pigment, and of other pigments removed, and establish their origins and dates.

Work done by Michelangelo *a secco* is cleaned differently. Because there is no carbonisation (the fusion created in *buon fresco*) the paint floats freely on the surface of the *intonaco*, so it must be fixed with a non-water-soluble solution, called Paraloid B 72.

Perhaps one reason that there is bad feeling – though in an increasingly small group of academics – is that the cleaning of the ceiling has forced us to re-evaluate Michelangelo and the history of Italian painting. He himself is directly responsible for some of the controversy about his work, and not only because he was its creator. . . .

His own evaluation of his painting makes us wonder about the newly cleaned Sistine Chapel ceiling. The image he projects of

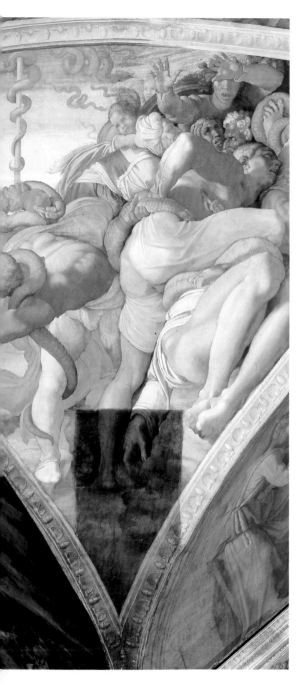

Detail from one of the spandrels showing an uncleaned patch and portions of the fictive architecture before and after cleaning.

Right *The Delphic Sibyl after cleaning.*

himself in his youthful Roman days is of an unhappy painter, unskilled and untutored. This is all well documented. He continually signs his letters, 'Michelangelo, sculptor in Rome', and this has a deliberate feel to it. Who then can blame the great Michelangelo scholars who have referred to his 'negative' style (Hibberd) or his 'poetry of sunset' (de Tolnay), the 'dominant tone (being) that of the fictive stone of the framework of architecture' (Freedberg), 'the darker colour scheme' (Wolfflin)? What have they had to go on? The ceiling has grown steadily darker over the years and Michelangelo tells us over and over again that he cannot paint.

Michelangelo seems to have been his own worst enemy. He was as hard on himself as he was on other people, perhaps harder. He was also very sure of his opinions. For someone with such a sense of colour, he certainly saw the world in terms of black and white. He is so strong an artist that he possesses a kind of moral authority. How could anyone possibly have guessed that Michelangelo was a terrible judge of his own work? I personally believe that many artists are. For centuries, Michelangelo has had scholars believing that he was a sculptor who put up a good fight against colour. He gives the impression of waging war against the tyranny of two dimensions, preferring the three dimensions of sculpture that denote freedom for him.

Now Michelangelo's painting has come out of the darkness with a vigour that is hard to believe. Far from being gloomy and melancholy, he seems to emerge as a person of tremendous positive energy. His colours sing and make strange harmonies. The volume and weight of his figures create contrapuntal rhythms with delicate tones of colour. He possesses the innate grace of the very strong.

The cleaning of the Sistine Chapel ceiling forces us to examine our tastes that reflect a preference for dark romanticism in art and artists. Angst is central to twentieth-century aesthetics, seen as a means of expressing the profound unconscious mind. Michelangelo is seen to be the prince of angst. In addition, our century like many others, including the Renaissance, values age in its cultural artefacts. We delight in the pleasure of ruins. We have a sense of wonder at the ageing process. The irony is that we try at all costs to avoid it in our bodies, but we esteem it in our art.

So why not let it be? Why not keep the Michelangelo that we know and love? Because in the Sistine Chapel we do not have a choice. It is not a matter of aesthetics. If we do not remove the poisonous substances that have eaten away at Michelangelo's greatest painting for five hundred years, future generations will see nothing but ghosts when they visit the chapel in time to come.

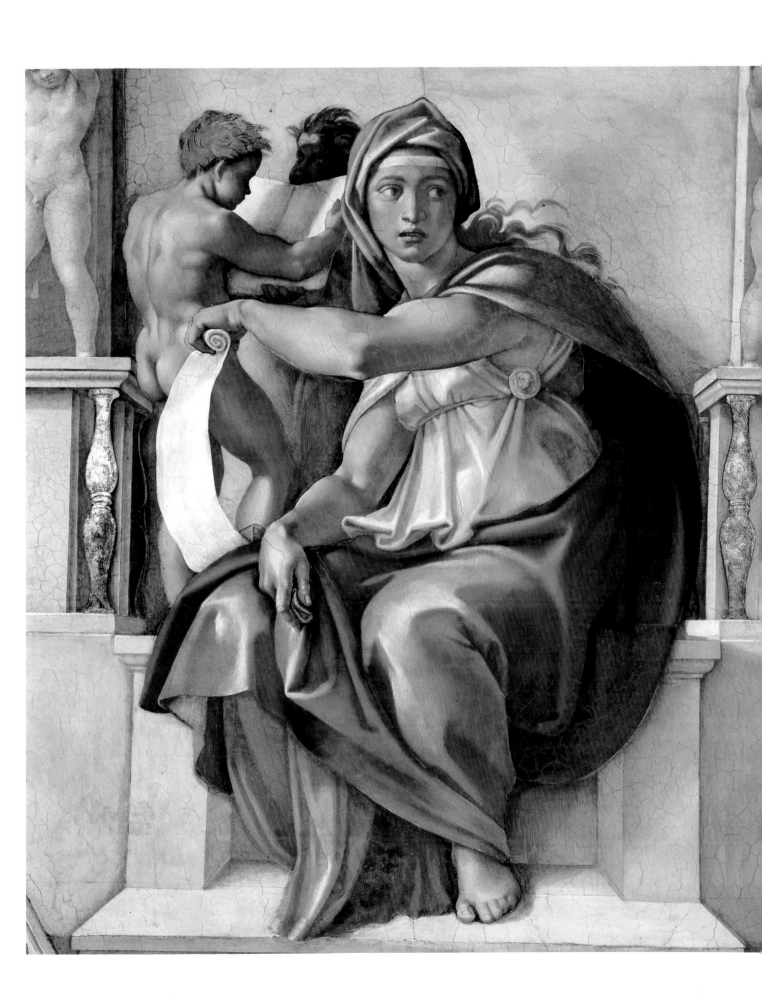

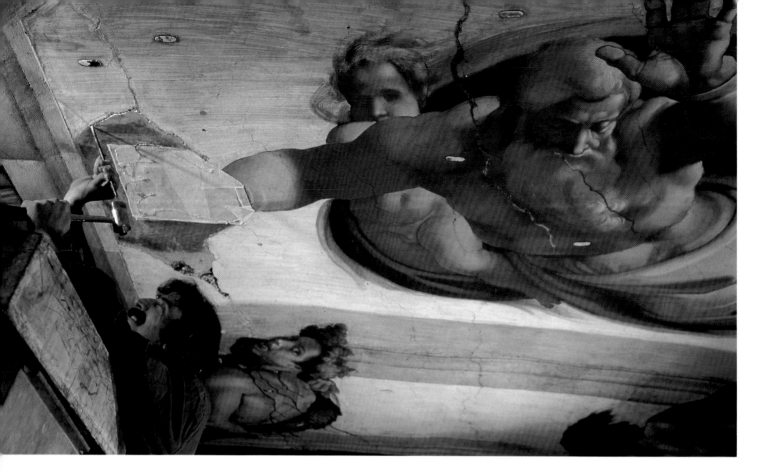

One of the Vatican team of restorers working on a crack in the ceiling.

The Vatican is now creating a micro-climate that will ensure stable ventilation and air circulation. Humidity will be controlled by a computerised system located under the flooring. The air, warmer than the cool stone walls, will no longer rise up to the ceiling on a convection current, bringing dust and dirt to rest on the frescoes. The heating in winter is already set at a lower temperature and the lighting has been radically altered, so that it shines away from the frescoes. Special carpet has been put in place outside the chapel, which removes dust from shoes.

But the real problem facing the future of the Sistine Chapel is that of people. It would be a tragedy if it went the way of another great work of art – the prehistoric paintings on the cave walls at Lascaux, almost destroyed by human breath and now closed forever to the general public. It would be painful and difficult to limit the number of people allowed into the chapel and this is not an option at the moment. (On one day in the summer of 1989, 19,000 visitors were recorded.) But there may be no other solution. At Lascaux, the authorities have employed expert copyists to recreate the ancient cave paintings on facsimile caves. The copy is marvellous. It is brilliant. It looks just like the real thing. But there is nobody alive who can, or would dare, to recreate the vision of Michelangelo. We had better take care of the one we have.

Before and after

The following pages illustrate details of the frescoes before and after cleaning.

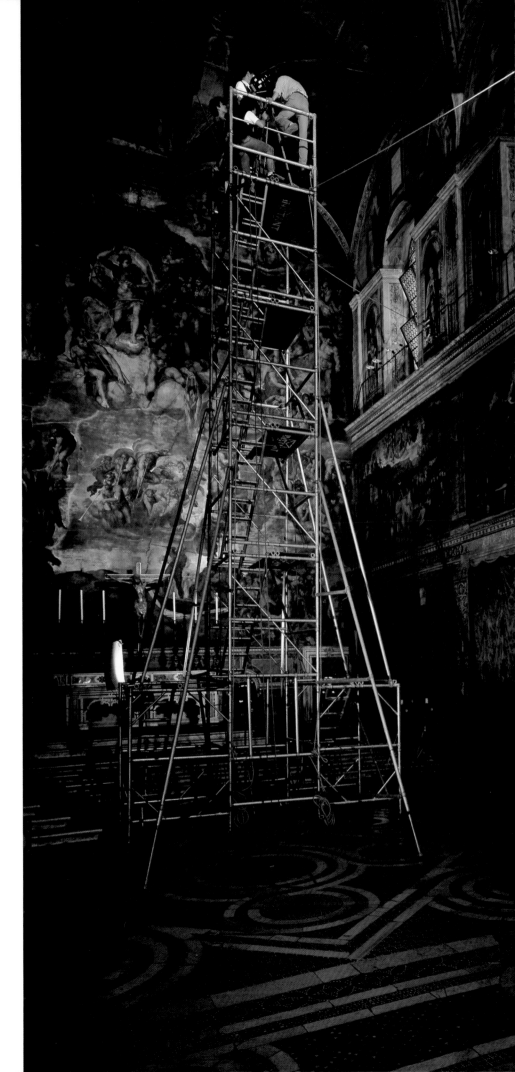

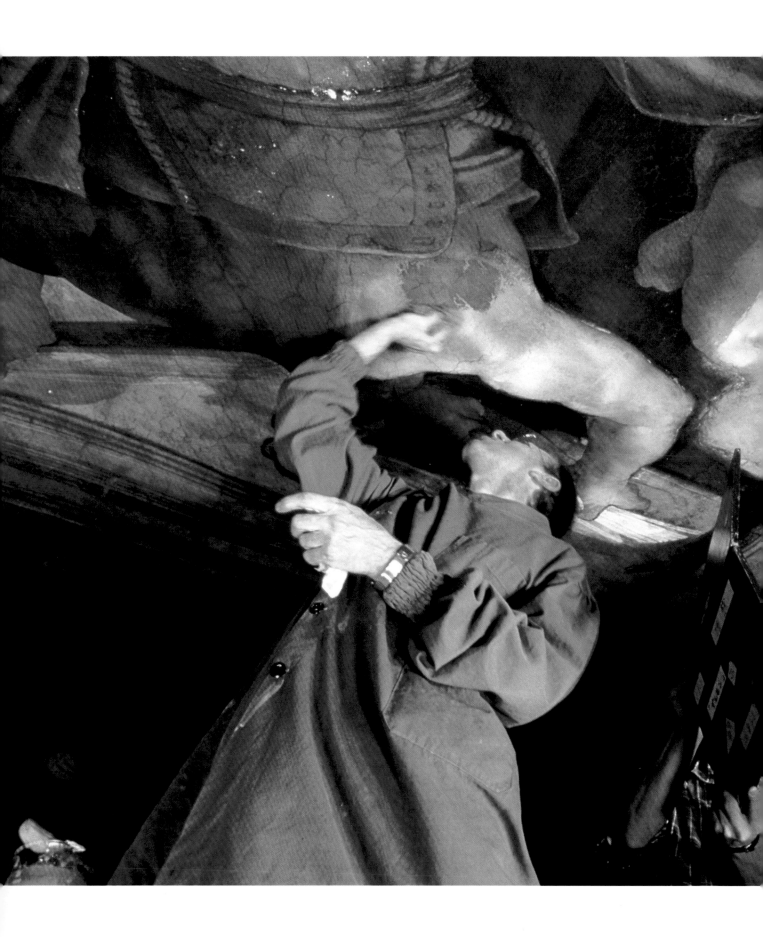

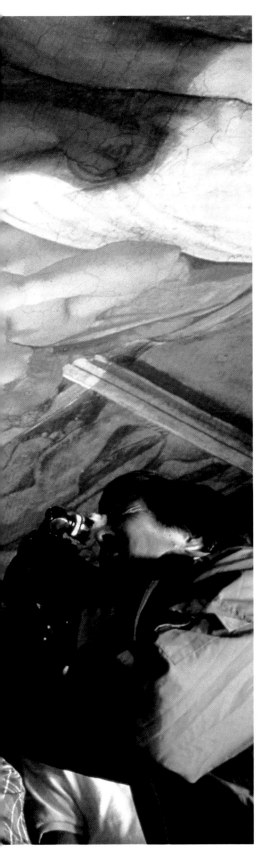

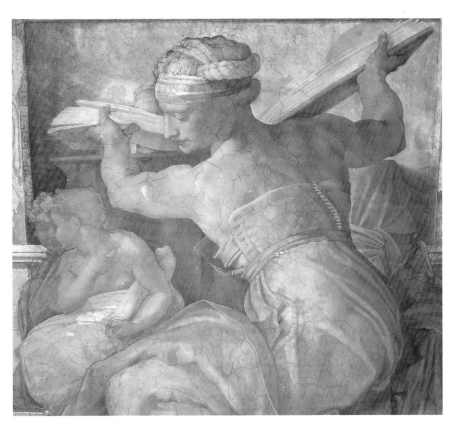

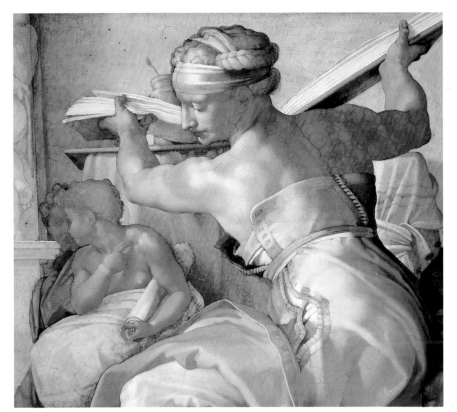

A member of the Nippon team of photographers records the cleaning of the Libyan Sibyl.

A detail before and after cleaning.

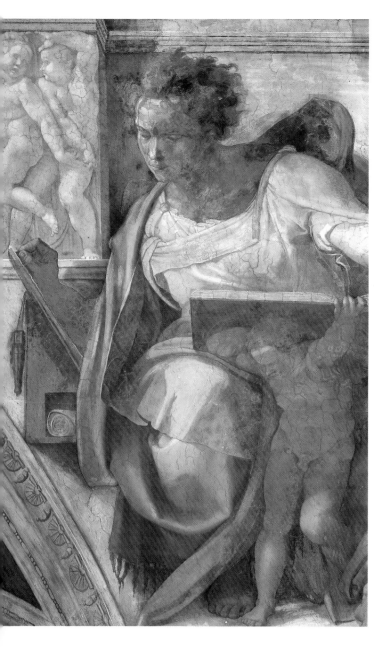
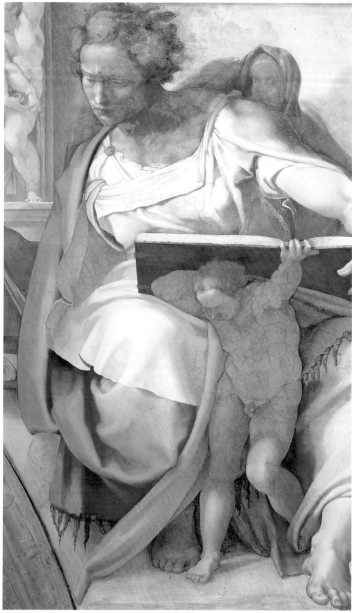

Details of the Prophet Daniel before and after cleaning.

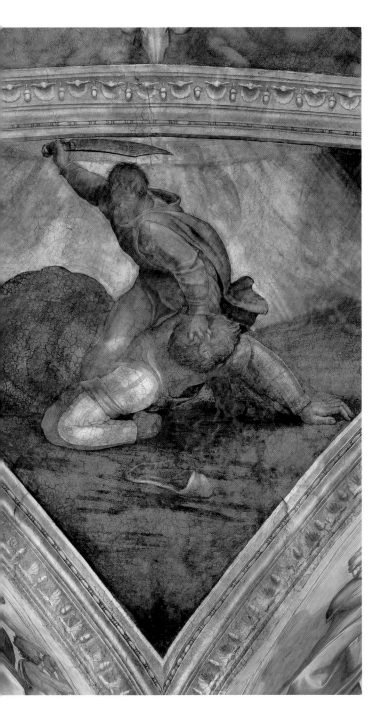
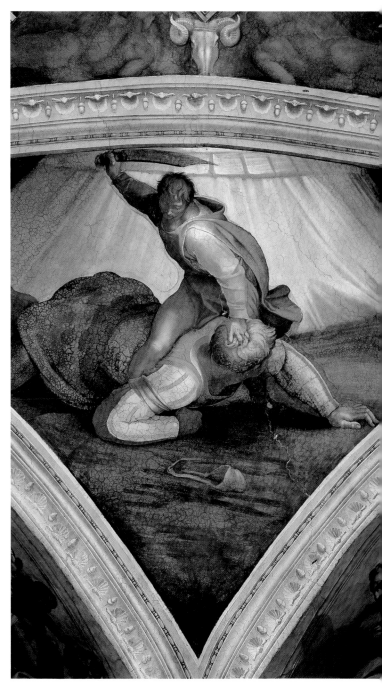

Detail of the spandrel David and Goliath
before and after cleaning.

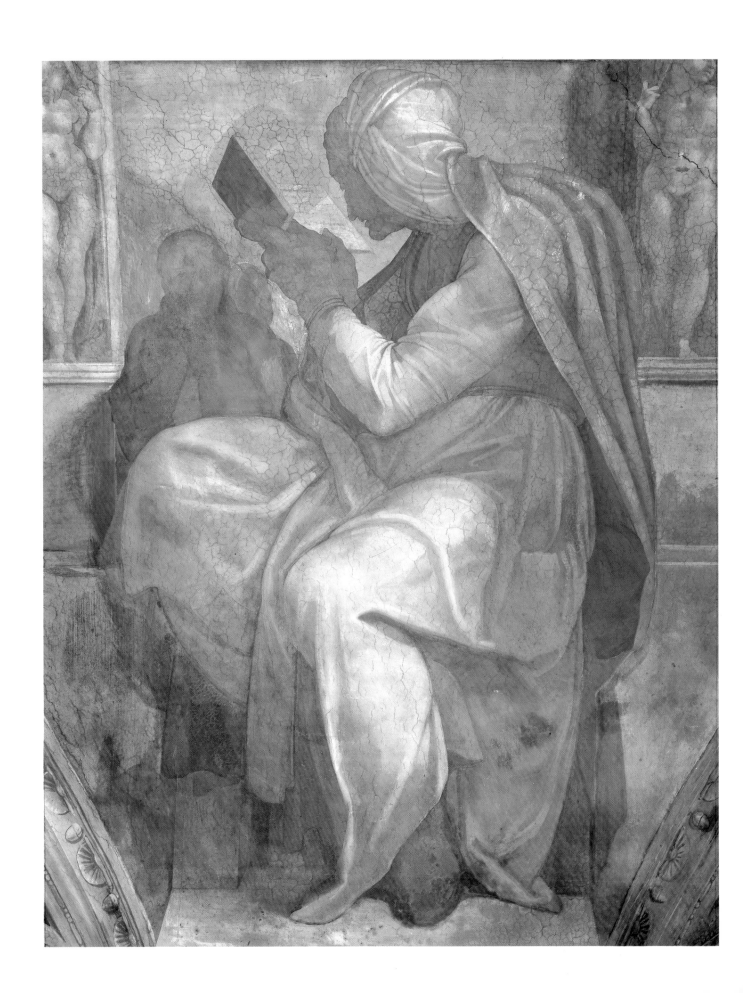

The Persian Sibyl before and after cleaning.

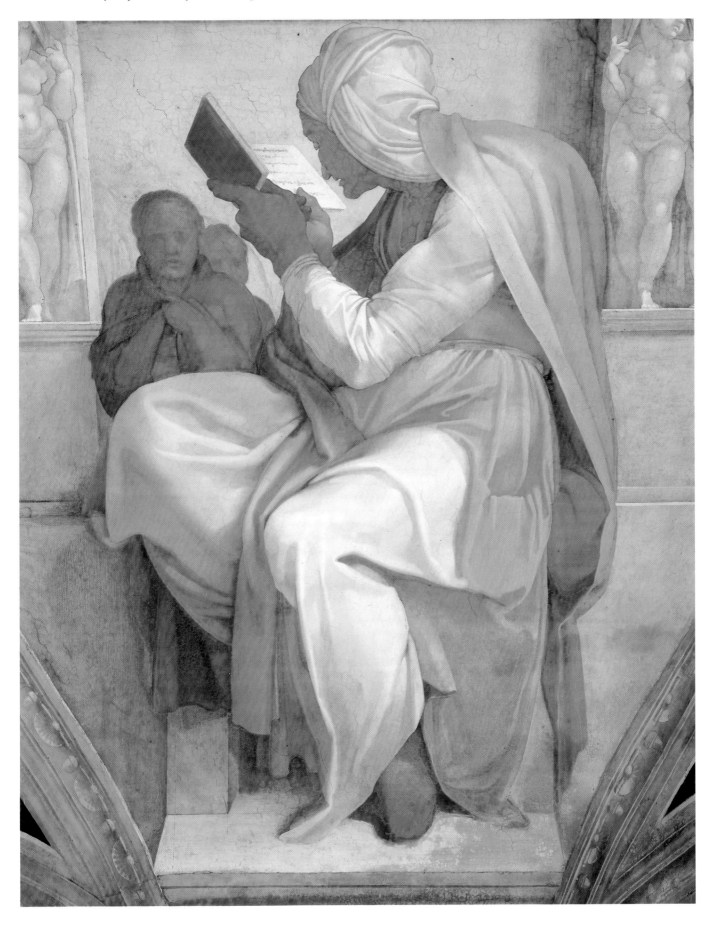

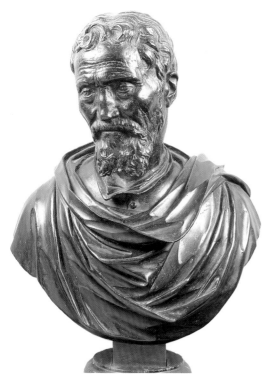

Bust of Michelangelo by Daniele da Volterra.

Impressions of Michelangelo

While still a young man, working in Lorenzo's household at the informal school under Bertoldo's supervision, Michelangelo had an experience that marked him for life, probably a result of other's jealousy. Always restless and provocative, he teased a fellow student mercilessly in front of the Masaccio frescoes in the Brancacci Chapel. The student, one Pietro Torrigiano, punched him so hard on the nose that it was crushed 'like a biscuit'. Michelangelo was certainly a person of extremes, who aroused extremes of emotion in others. That battered, broken nose is the most distinctive physical feature of Michelangelo's face, as seen from the surviving portraits of him. His friend Condivi gives a vivid description of Michelangelo's face in his biography of the artist, below.

Portrait of Michelangelo in the Casa Buonarroti, Florence. Artist unknown.

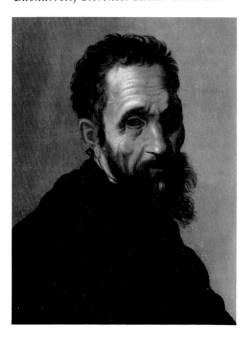

Michelangelo is of sound constitution. He is bony and wiry rather than fat and fleshy and he is naturally healthy as well through exercise and abstinence from sex and food, even though he was sickly as a boy and has been seriously ill twice. For years he has found it painful to urinate, and if it were not for the diligence of Messer Realdo, the problem would have developed into stones. He has always had good facial colour, and his stature is as follows:

He is of medium height, broad across the shoulders, the rest of his body in proportion and more slender than anything else. The front part of his skull is round so that over the ears it makes a half circle and a sixth. His temples stick out beyond his ears and his ears beyond his cheekbones, and these beyond the rest. All this infers that his head is large in relation to the size of his face. From the front his head looks square and the nose is a bit squashed, not naturally but because a man called Torrigiano de' Torrigiani, a beastly arrogant man, almost tore off the cartilage of his nose with his fist, and he was brought home as if for dead. . . .

His lips are thin but the bottom one is a bit fuller and if you see him in profile it sticks out a bit. His chin goes well with the features already mentioned. In profile, his forehead sticks out further than his nose which has a little bump in the middle but is otherwise almost flat. He has hardly any eyebrows, and his eyes are on the small side, the colour of horn but changeable with glimmers of yellow and blue. The ears are just right, the hair and beard black, except that now that he is seventy-nine, they are tinged with grey. The beard is forked, between four and five fingers long, not very full, as can be partly seen in his portrait.

Sonnet for Giovanni da Pistoia, Chancellor of the Florence Academy, 1509-1510, composed while at work on the Sistine Chapel ceiling. NOTE: *The translation renders the sense of the colloquial, though now archaic Italian, and does not always follow the line order of the original.*

I'ho già fatto un gozzo in questo stento

*My belly is shoved so far up under my chin
that it makes me look as though I've got myself a goitre
Just like those cats from Lombardy get from drinking bad water,
(or wherever it is that they come from).
My beard faces skywards and the nape of my neck
is wedged on my spine
so that I've got the puffed-up bosom of a shrew.
My face is richly carpeted with a thick layer of paint from my brush,
and my loins are pushed up into my stomach
so that I'm forced to lean backwards to stay upright
as though I'm horseback riding and I can't see where to put my feet.
My skin is stretched in front and wrinkled in back
and I'm stretched like a bow from Syria.
It's no wonder then that my sense of judgement is way off course.
Giovanni, please come to the rescue of me, and my dead art.
I don't feel that I'm in the right place and I am no painter.*

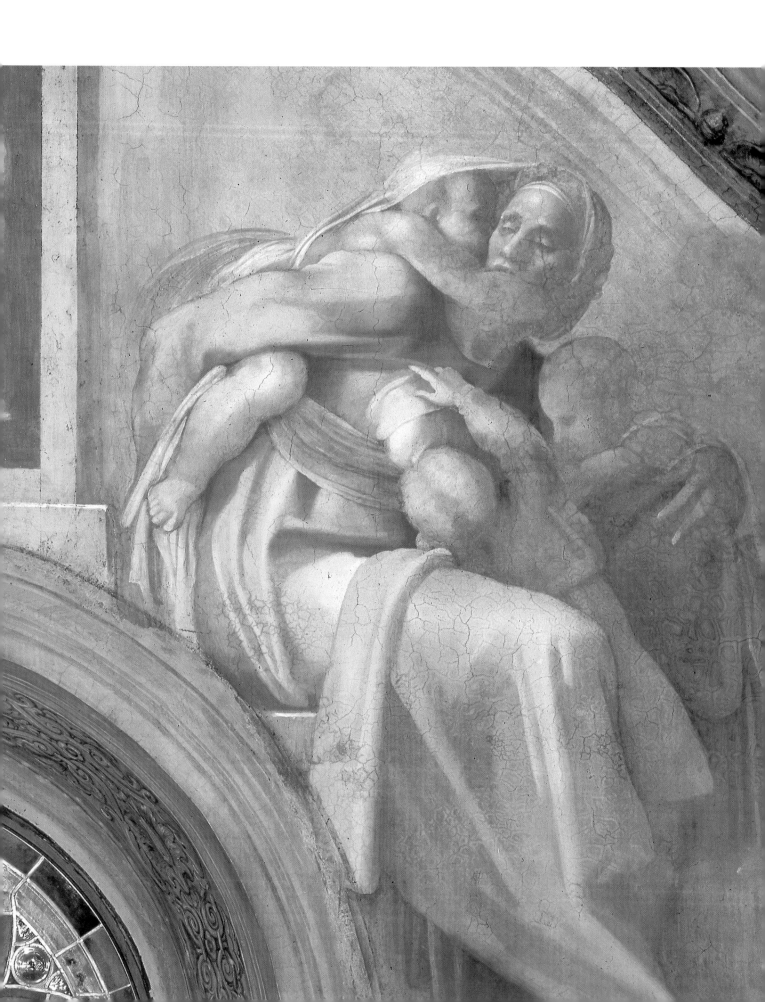

8 Michelangelo, Man and Artist

Even if Michelangelo had never touched a brush or a chisel again after descending wearily from the scaffold in 1512, the painting of the Sistine Chapel ceiling would have assured him a place in history. It is a landmark in the long, complicated story of art – a symbol of its age like the Sphinx in Egypt, the Greek Parthenon or the Taj Mahal in India. Because it is the work of one person, it says something about all of us. Yet it is also simple. We feel an immediacy that is electric. The charged few inches between the hands of God and Adam grow visibly in the huge space between the ground and the painting itself, twenty metres (sixty-five feet) above us. We are drawn to this part of the painting, for it is the moment of life. Whether we are of any religion or none, we are moved by the intensity of this man's vision of a perfect world, a world without chaos, where everything is preordained and interconnecting.

The story might at first seem too specific. Man's original sin and eventual redemption through Christ might mean very little to those who believe in other gods, or none at all. But Michelangelo tells us that despair and weakness can be transcended. He makes his belief in the goodness of mankind very clear in his celebration of human beauty. We are shown by example the creative power and energy of our uniquely human spirit manifested by God in His creation.

When Michelangelo finished his work for Pope Julius II, he was thirty-seven and old before his time. The rigours of painting in the impossible posture of the 'Syrian bow' had reduced his body to a state of exhaustion. His joints ached, his eyes were strained, his patience was all but gone.

But he was famous. He was admired by most of his contemporaries and envied by the others. His talent was considered so extraordinary that it was frightening, hence the new word used to describe his work – *terribiltà*. His powers of concentration and commitment were legendary, and his personal style became the stuff of myth in his own lifetime, adding to the aura of otherworldliness that he possessed in full measure. His carelessness towards his own physical well-being became notorious. Vasari, his biographer in later years, has described how the

Detail from the lunette of Asa, Josaphat and Joram.

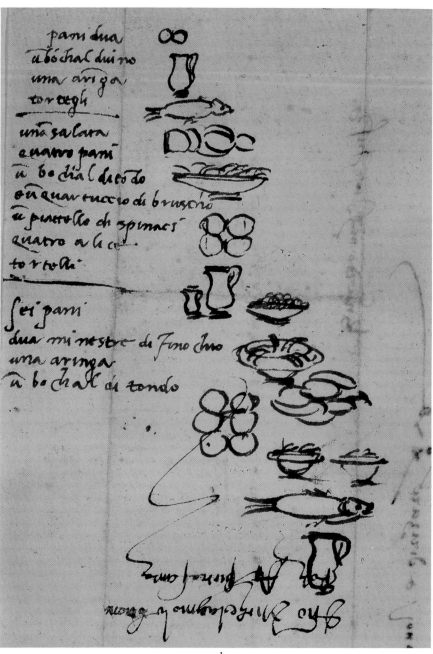

A shopping list in Michelangelo's handwriting, with drawings for a servant who was possibly illiterate. It includes herring, stewed fennel, a dish of spinach, bread rolls and a jug of wine.

artist lived for months in the same 'buskins', or long boots (Condivi refers to his breeches). He recalls that when these were removed, the skin followed!

Michelangelo did not, evidently, care for the pleasures of the material world. He lived mostly inside his head and the landscape of his own thoughts was infinitely more interesting to him than the comforts of his home, or anyone else's. He held the belief, central to his faith and the legacy of Savonarola's teaching, that the flesh must be mortified. Its pleasures were meaningless in comparison with the purity of the soul. It is perhaps this fierce physical self-denial that helps to fuel the suppressed energy flowing unimpeded into his art. It was only much later in his life that the love for other people truly enriched his solitude.

Fortunately, both for us and for Michelangelo, other projects crowded into his life and filled the vacuum left by the completion of the Sistine Chapel ceiling. Work, not human relationships, was the centre and meaning of his existence. He was involved in artistic creation to the end.

Six days before he died, he was still hacking away at the *Rondanini Pietà*, dissatisfied and impatient with what Dylan Thomas referred to as his 'craft and sullen art'. The years after the painting of the Sistine Chapel ceiling were very busy. Some of his greatest work was accomplished in this long period. He became one of the greatest architects of the time and created designs for buildings in both Florence and Rome of peerless serenity and balance.

His long obsession with the tomb of Julius II continued to

Michelangelo's drawing for the fortifications of Florence, 1528–29.

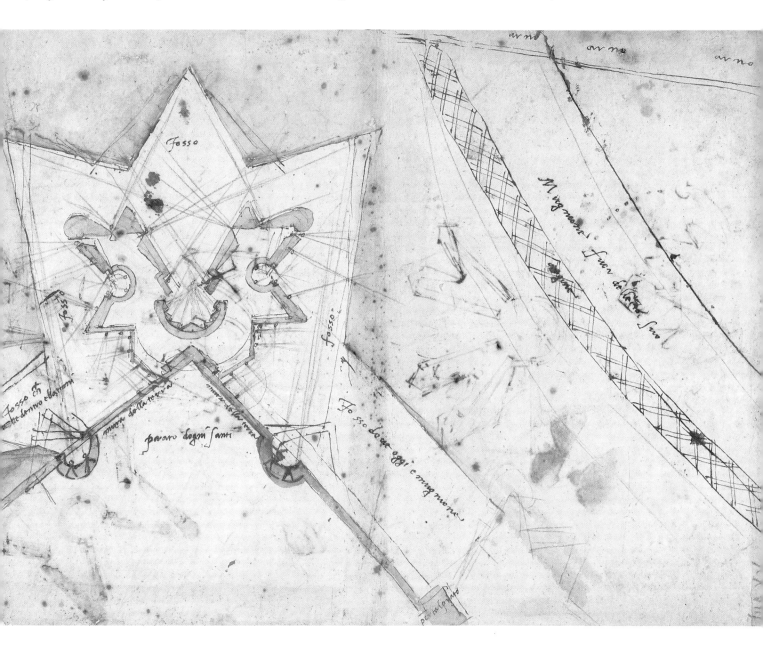

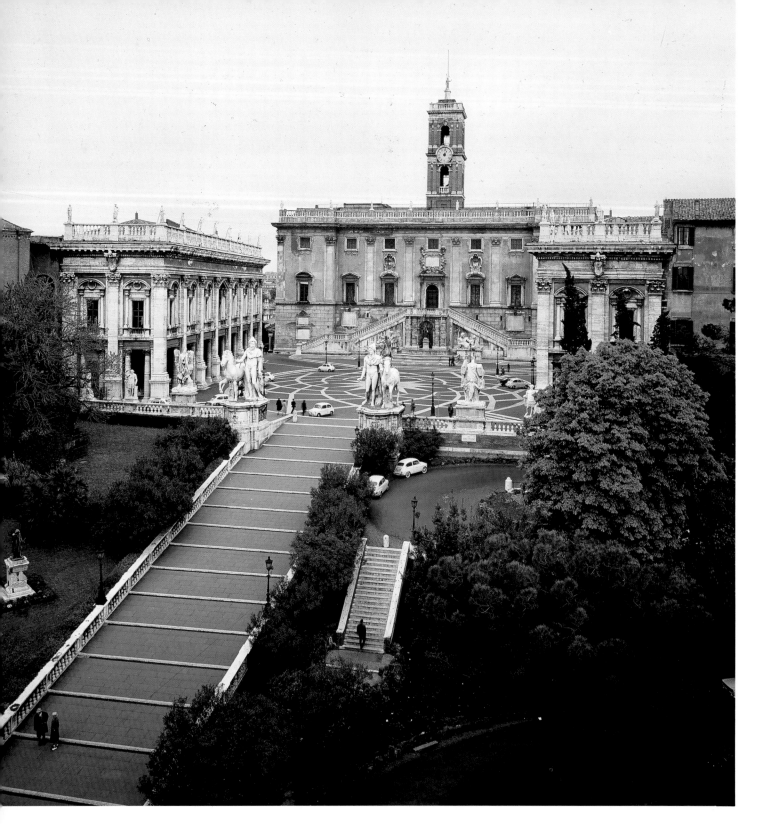

The Campidoglio in Rome, the piazza and its surrounding buildings and formal stairs were designed by Michelangelo, 1546–50.

haunt him, until a much reduced version of the original was erected in the Church of San Pietro in Vincoli in 1545. But he worked for other patrons as imperious in their ways as his old patron Julius, who had died in 1513, only months after the ceiling was finished. The Papacy passed from the old della Rovere family to the Medici and they continued to employ him in architectural and sculptural projects.

Old rivalries ceased to plague him and feed his nagging paranoia. Raphael, the favoured and charming young painter, died too young in 1520, leaving frescoes behind him in the Vatican which paid homage to the master Michelangelo, who had looked down on the handsome dandy. Raphael pays generous tribute to Michelangelo in his portrait in the papal *Stanze*. Raphael's frescoes in the Church of Santa Maria della Pace in Rome are an even deeper reflection of this admiration, as again Vasari noted. Bramante, Michelangelo's other old rival, died in 1514, and Michelangelo himself was in 1547 appointed official but unpaid architect of St Peter's by Pope Paul III of the Farnese family. This must have occasioned some ironical amusement to Michelangelo, after all his early torments fifty years before.

In the years after painting the Sistine Chapel ceiling,

The tomb of Giuliano de' Medici in the New Sacristy of the Church of San Lorenzo, Florence, 1520–34.

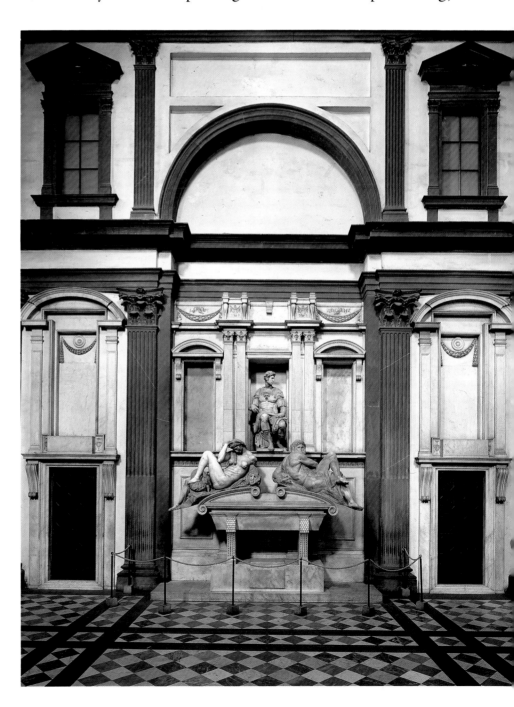

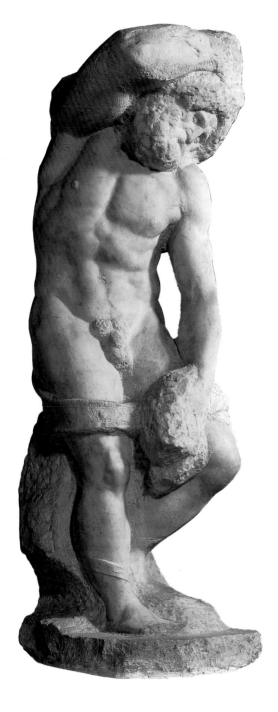

Bearded Slave *by Michelangelo,*
1520–23. Marble, unfinished.

Michelangelo created sculpture of greater emotional intensity than ever. He produced the *Moses* and the *Bound Slaves* designed for Julius's tomb (but not destined to be united in that work), the *Deposition of Christ* (designed for his own tomb), the *Rondanini Pietà* and many other great works. But the reluctant painter was not finished with painting. He was to fulfil two more important fresco commissions, the *Last Judgement* in 1536-41, in the Sistine Chapel, and the *Conversion of Paul* and the *Crucifixion of Peter* in 1542-50, in the Pope's private Pauline Chapel in the Vatican.

The horrors of the sack of Rome, which had subjected the city and the Vatican and its inhabitants to atrocities by marauding armies of Charles V in 1527, and the plague that followed, had a devastating effect on the artist as well as on the stricken city and the Papacy. As Michelangelo grew older, suffering from the agonies of bladder stones and aching bones, his religion was to become even more important to him. But the terrible events he witnessed darkened his view of mankind profoundly.

The *Last Judgement* on the altar wall of the Sistine Chapel had been commissioned by another Pope, Clement VII, and upon his sudden death his successor Paul III – who was a great art lover – had renewed the project intended to celebrate the Resurrection of Christ. Michelangelo permitted two of his own earlier lunettes and pendentives from the ceiling to be destroyed, and also two windows were bricked in. Four of the ancestors of Christ, two portraits of canonised Popes, Perugino's fresco of the *Assumption of the Virgin* – and two valuable sources of light – were thus lost. The *Last Judgement* is a most remarkable work. But it is only necessary here to note the change of heart it shows. The youthful, optimistic Michelangelo has become gloomy and sorrowful.

There are probably many reasons for this. He felt the onset of age, with its infirmities, and it pointed his thoughts towards his own death. His father, Lodovico, died aged ninety in 1534. The threat to the Church from outside must have intensified his belief, but may also have made him question it. The Church was experiencing a re-evaluation of its practices that must have been profoundly disturbing to its faithful flock. The hell-fire sermons of the priest Savonarola were still ringing in Michelangelo's ears and he indeed complained of this nightmare. The new puritanical atmosphere in Rome, emphasizing human sinfulness, inevitably had an effect on his earlier belief that Man's achievement before God was both beautiful and valid. The conflict, suffering and fear that he had observed since the sack of Rome must have made the idea of a merciful God less easy to accept.

But there is a more human element to the story, although it may seem a contradiction. In 1532, at the age of fifty-seven, Michelangelo had met the young and handsome Tommaso de' Cavalieri. He became obsessed with the beauty of the young nobleman and, possibly for the first time, he was consumed by

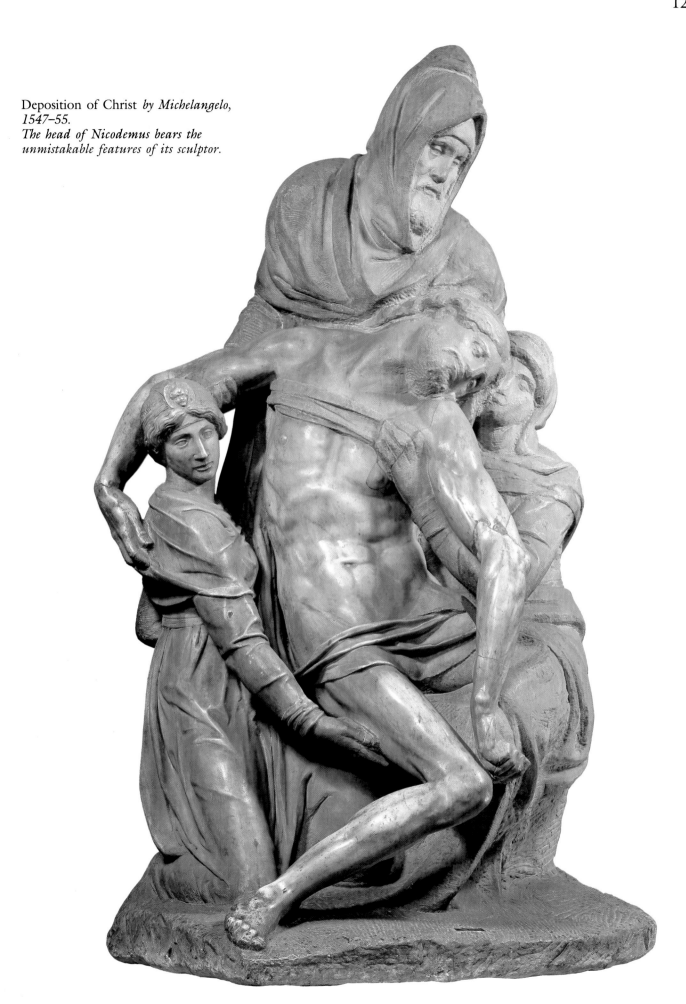

Deposition of Christ *by Michelangelo,*
1547–55.
The head of Nicodemus bears the
unmistakable features of its sculptor.

feeling for another person, rather than for his art. He wrote many ardent and emotional letters and poems to Tommaso.

The courtly poems that he wrote display a lyrical use of language. He declares himself to be a 'prisoner of his armed cavalier' (*resto prigion d'un cavalier armato*), a pun on Tommaso's name, but seems to be in love more with the idea of love than with its object. Still, this is a new Michelangelo. It is improbable that this love was ever expressed physically, for Michelangelo was an ascetic who lived most comfortably in his mind. Condivi writes of Michelangelo's sexual abstinence in his memoir. But the strength of his emotion was enough to change his self-absorbed way of life, and must certainly have made him feel more vulnerable, as is shown in the poem he wrote to Tommaso in 1532.

Four years later he met the noblewoman Vittoria Colonna, the Marchioness of Pescara, and she too affected him deeply. A fervent Christian and an accomplished poet herself, she was known for her wisdom and piety. Her religious discipline was strict and uncompromising and her belief included no possibility of changing one's destiny. This view would have contributed to the darkening of Michelangelo's spiritual vision, so powerfully depicted in the *Last Judgement*. It was to her that he wrote what is often taken to be a statement of his artistic philosophy in the sonnet (*Rime* 151, quoted on page 134) that begins: *Non ha l'ottimo artista alcun concetto. . .*

'Even the greatest artist has no idea that is not already buried deep within the marble. . . .'

This poem expresses one element of Michelangelo's belief that was ever present: that his talent was an instrument of God's will.

When Vittoria died in 1547, Michelangelo was grief-stricken and dazed by the loss. According to Condivi, he loved her so much that he berated himself for kissing her hand when he paid his last respects, rather than kissing her forehead or her face, acting with courtliness rather than passion. His life was never again to be graced with the love that passes *per acqua e foco l'alme a lieti giorni* ('through water and flames to happier days'). The brief lightening of loneliness came to an end with her passing, although Tommaso was with him in his last days, seventeen years later, ever the true and faithful friend.

When Michelangelo died at eleven o'clock in the evening on 18 February 1564, he was almost ninety. In his will he left 'his soul to God, his body to the earth, and his possessions to his nearest relatives', according to Vasari. He was buried with pomp and ceremony in the Church of Sant' Apostoli in Rome, which had long ago adopted him as a favoured citizen. But with a fitting strangeness that had surrounded Michelangelo all his life, his body was smuggled out of Rome by his nephew Lionardo on

The Last Judgement *by Michelangelo, right, fresco on the west wall of the Sistine Chapel, 1536–41.*

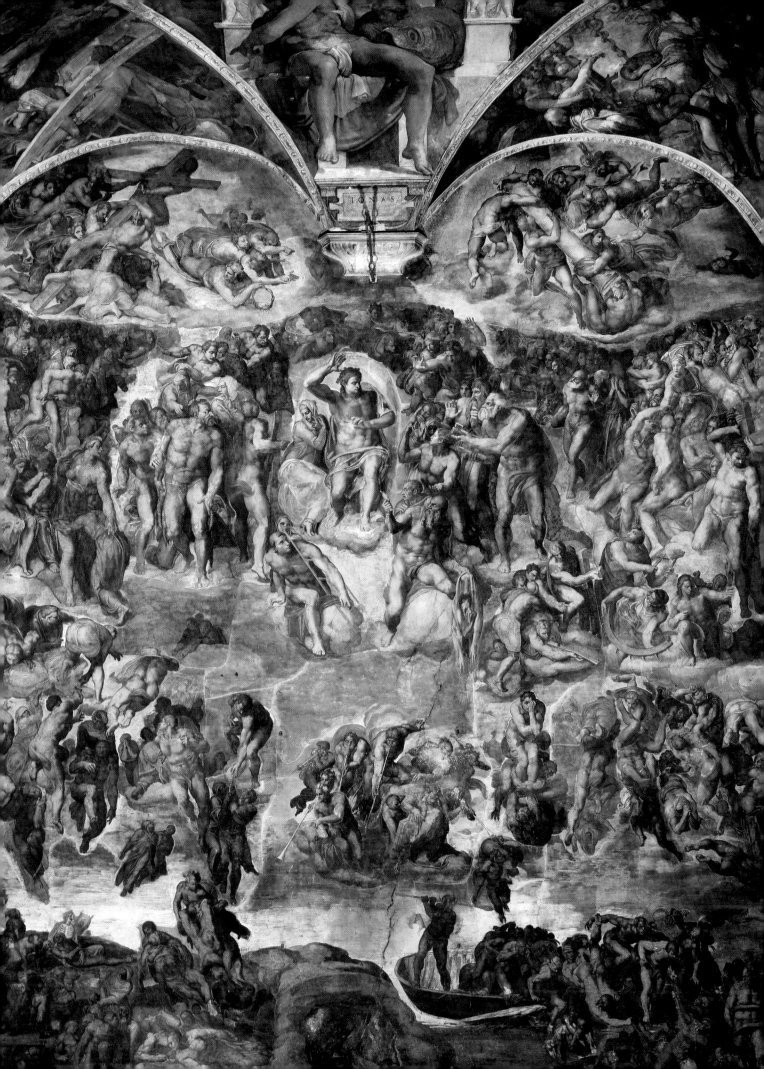

132

10 March and spirited away to Florence. The people of Florence had reclaimed what was truly theirs. Their brave, noble son was laid to rest for ever on 12 March in the Church of Santa Croce, under whose shadow he had played as a boy. A solemn funeral mass was held in the presence of the city dignitaries in the Medici Church of San Lorenzo on 14 July 1564.

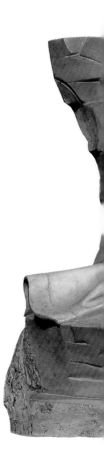

Perhaps Michelangelo's most famous statue, the Pietà *in St Peter's, Rome, assured his reputation as an artist. Commissioned by Jean de Villiers de la Groslaye, it was the only work he signed himself. It is hard not to identify the young Virgin with an idealised portrait of the artist's mother, who died when Michelangelo was only six. Whether this is so or not, the image expresses immense grief and loss.*

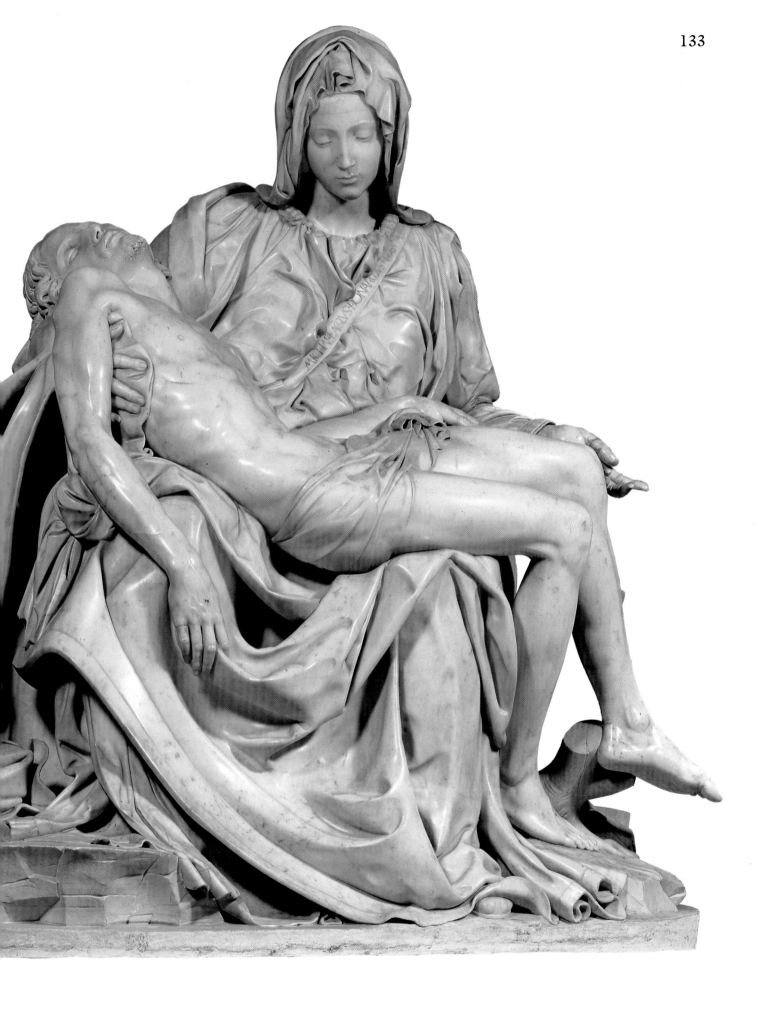

9 *The Evidence of the Sonnets*

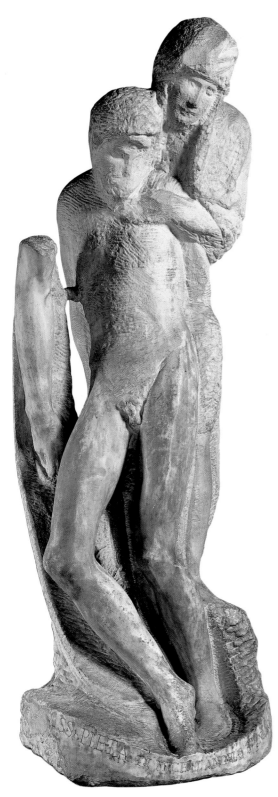

The Spirit within the Stone

Michelangelo was an articulate man, who seems to have felt almost as easy with language as with marble or paint. He wrote accomplished poetry in the courtly, Renaissance madrigal style. This passionate poetry is admired by scholars, but loses a great deal in translation. The language of the sonnets is formal and condensed. I have chosen a few that represent his range of poetic power, but have not translated them lyrically (nor always line for line), since I want to render their meaning as simply as possible. I have referred in the bibliography to various classic versions.

On the death of Vittoria Colonna, after c.1528

Se 'l mio rozzo martello i duri sassi

If my rough hammer makes human forms out of the hard stone
it is because of He who urges and guides its action.
Only one divine being lives in Heaven
and He creates beauty without human help.
No hammer is forged entirely out of nothing
except by the Divine Carpenter.
The hammer's blow is strongest when it is raised from on high,
and her soul that helped to create mine, has reached these heights
While my own imperfect hammer must remain so
unless God, the Divine maker, gives me His help.

The Rondanini Pietà, 1555–64.
Michelangelo was working on this marble statue only days before his death. Problems with the piece are evident in the ambiguity of the forms and the mystery of the disembodied arm, finished to a high polish, though the 'idea buried deep within the marble' emerges forcefully.
Michelangelo seems to be contemplating his own approaching death in this work, which conveys feelings of compassion and vulnerability.

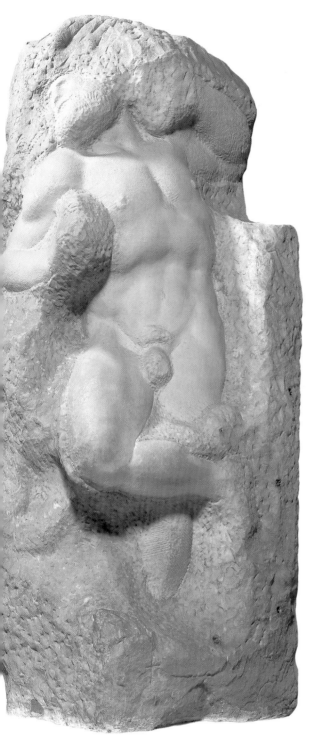

Awakening Slave *by Michelangelo,*
1520–23. Marble.

One of Michelangelo's rough sketches with
dimensions and instructions for the
stonemasons who would prepare the block
of marble for cutting.

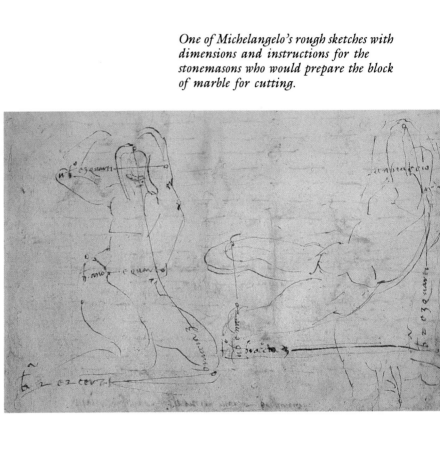

To Vittoria Colonna

Non ha l'ottimo artista alcun concetto

Even the greatest artist has no idea that is not already buried
deep within the marble.
And the spell of that idea can only be broken
when the hand obeys the mind.
The evil that I escape and the good to which I aspire
are hidden in you, Lady of great refinement.
And my art is not great enough to achieve my goal.
Your beauty and your severity are not to blame for my problem.
Nor is Love or Fate.
I am in charge of my destiny.
Because though you carry compassion and death
within your worthy heart
my unworthy talent knows only of death.

On Age, Love and Death
To Tommaso de' Cavalieri, 1532

S'i' avessi creduto al primo sguardo

If I had thought, with his first glance
that I could renew myself in the scorching heat of his burning gaze,
Ardently desiring to know his soul which, phoenix-like,
has ripened my old age,
I would have come to him before,
With the speed of a stag, a lynx or a leopard.
Now I want to run but am too slow.
Why should I mourn any more when I can see my own peace,
rest and happiness
inside this happy angel's eyes.
It is better to have seen him and heard him now
so that we can share our wings to fly upwards in pursuit of his virtue.

To Tommaso de' Cavalieri, c.1534

Veggio nel tuo bel viso signor mio

I learn things from your beautiful face my lord
that can never be spoken of in this life.
Your soul, still clothed in flesh,
soars repeatedly towards the face of God.
The uncharitable mockery of the low and vicious
cannot pollute the power of my love, faith, and true desire
which are the most important things to me.
All the wonders that we see on earth
resemble that divine being that created us.
We have no memories or evidence of Paradise in any other place
except in my love for you that helps me rise towards God,
my death made sweeter through my love.

🖜 10 Sixteenth-Century Voices

19 August 1497

Dearest Father etc....

This is to let you know that Buonarroto (Michelangelo's favourite younger brother, visiting Rome after the death of his stepmother Lucrezia) *arrived here on Friday, and as soon as I knew I went to the inn to meet him. He told me how things were with you, and said that the Consiglio* (Lodovico's brother-in-law, the haberdasher Consiglio Antonio Cisti, who was owed ninety gold florins by Michelangelo's father) *was being a bore and that he wouldn't agree on anything and wanted to have you arrested. I'm telling you that you should see your way to paying him something and let me know what's left over and I'll send it to you if you haven't got it, even though I myself have hardly anything, like I already said. I'll try to get it so you don't have to take anything out of the Monte* (bank) *like Buonarroto is talking about. Don't be surprised that I'm writing you such a tetchy letter because I have very strong feelings about some important matters in my own life that have nothing to do with this.*

I was supposed to do a figure for Piero de' Medici (Lorenzo the Magnificent's son, banished from Florence in 1494, two years after Lorenzo's death) *and bought the marble but I didn't start on it because he didn't do what he promised. So I'm on my own, doing a figure for my own pleasure. I bought a piece of marble for five ducats and it wasn't any good so I've thrown away that money, but then I bought another piece, another five ducats, and this work is just for me so you'd better believe me when I say that I'm spending money and wearing myself out. Still, you'll get what you ask for from me even if I have to sell myself as a slave.*

Buonarroto is safely arrived now and has gone back to his inn. He has a room and he's comfortable and has everything he wants, no matter how long he stays. I haven't got the space to put him up because I'm staying with people, but I won't let him go without anything he needs. I'm healthy, as I hope this letter finds you.

Michelangniolo in Rome

There is a funny postscript to this letter, in Lodovico's handwriting, that shows his relief at Michelangelo's generosity: '*Dicie aiutarmi paghare Consiglio.*' 'He says he'll help me pay Consiglio.'

Note: the spelling or rendering of names was very flexible at the time. Michelangelo also signs himself Michelangelus or Michelangniolo.

138

Extract from a long letter to Michelangelo from Lodovico, 21 July 1508. Note that the contract for the Sistine Chapel ceiling was signed in May 1508.

21 July 1508

Dearest Son,

It seems to me that you're overdoing it and it upsets me that you're ill and unhappy and I'd pay a lot to see you get out of this job (the Sistine Chapel) *because if you feel so negative you won't do a very good job. . . .*

August 1508

Most reverend Father,

I've had a letter from a nun who says that she's our aunt and she says that she's very poor and in very great need and she wants charity from me. So, I'm sending you five ducats and I want you to give her four and a half. Please tell Buonarroto to use the half that's left over to buy some varnish from either Francesco Granacci or another painter. Get however much it will buy for the money. I want the best to be found in Florence. If there isn't any, don't worry about it. I think that this so-called nun who claims to be our aunt is in the convent of San Giuliano. I'd like you to go and see if it's true that she's really in such great need because there's something in her tone that I don't quite like. If the story is untrue, use the money yourself. I've nothing else to say for the moment because I'm not sure about my plans. I'll let you know as soon as I'm sure.

Your Michelangniolo, sculptor in Rome

27 January 1509

Dear Father,

. . . I'm still in a fix because I haven't had a cent from this Pope in a year and I can't really ask him for anything as my work doesn't deserve it as it's not going very well. That's the trouble with this work. It's not my profession. I'm wasting my time without a good result. Lord help me. If you need money go to the Spedalingo and make him give you up to fifteen ducats, and let me know what's left over. . . .

Your Michelangniolo in Rome

June 1509

Most reverend Father,

I hear from your last letter that people are saying that I'm dead. It's not all that important because I'm actually very much alive. But let them say what they want and don't talk about me to anyone because there are some really bad types around. I intend to work as hard as I can. I haven't had any money from the Pope in thirteen months now, but I think that I'll have some in a month and a half. In any case, I will at least have made good use of what I've already received. If he doesn't give me any, I'll have to borrow money to come home because I haven't a bean. Anyway, at least I can't be robbed. Please God that things improve. If you need money go to Santa Maria Nuova to the Spedalingo like I already told you to do. I have nothing else to say. I'm feeling very unhappy here and I'm not in good health and I'm exhausted. I haven't got anyone to look after me and I'm penniless.

Michelangniolo, sculptor in Rome

7 September 1510

Dearest Father,

I was very upset to hear that Buonarroto was ill. However as soon as you read this, go to the Spedalingo and make him give you the fifty or a hundred ducats that you need. Make sure you have enough and that you're not wanting. Take note that I'm waiting here for five hundred ducats, and as much again from the Pope that I've already earned. He was supposed to give it to me to pay for the scaffold for the other part of my work, and he's left here without leaving me any instructions. I've written him a letter. I don't know what will happen. I'd have come as soon as I received your news, but if I left without permission, the Pope would have a fit, and I'd lose what I'm owed. Don't forget that if Buonarroto is ill, let me know, because if you want, I can be there in two days flat because people are more important than money. Let me know because I'm in a state.

On 7 September,
Your Michelangniolo in Rome

---

21 August 1512

Buonarroto

I received your letter to which I'm replying briefly as I have no time . . . I can't come home because I must finish the job, which I hope to do by the end of September. It's a big job so I don't know how I'll do it in fifteen days. Anyway, as long as it's finished by All Saint's Day, it will be all right, if I don't drop dead beforehand. I'm in a rush because it seems as though I've been here for a thousand years.

Michelangniolo, sculptor in Rome

Early October 1512

Dear Father,

I gather from your last letter that you paid back your debt of forty ducats to the Spedalingo. You did well and when you feel that things are going wrong again, please let me know. I finished the chapel that I was painting and the Pope is well pleased. Other things aren't turning out so well and I blame the times we live in for the fact that conditions are so inhospitable to art. I won't see you this All Saints Day because it's not up to me and there isn't time anyway. Try to live as best you can and don't get worked up about anything. Nothing else.

Your Michelangniolo, sculptor in Rome

Note by Paris de Grassis, papal master of ceremonies, 31 October 1512

Vesperae in vigilia omnium sanctorum. . . . Hodie primum capella nostra, pingi finita, aperta est.

Vespers on the eve of All Saints Day. . . . Today is the first day our chapel is open, the painting is finished.

To his nephew, Buonarroto's son

4 September 1546

Lionardo

You wrote me a tract as long as a Bible over a triviality only to annoy me. About the money, the money (sic), *please just write to me about what needs to be done. Just work it out between yourselves and spend it on what you need most. Nothing else is new with me and I haven't got time to write.*

Michelangniolo in Rome

To his nephew, Buonarroto's son

Lionardo

I read from your latest letter that you have brought your new wife home and that you are very happy. . . . Live well and be careful because there are more widows than widowers.

Michelangniolo Buonarroti in Rome

March 1554

Lionardo

I had a letter from you last week where you describe the happiness that you continue to enjoy with Cassandra, about which we must thank God and even more so because it's such a rare thing. Give her my best and if she wants anything from here let me know. About the baby you expect, it seems suitable to me to name a boy after your father (who had died in 1528) *and a girl after our mother* (who died in 1481) *that is, Buonarroto and Francesca. . . . Nothing else is new. Look after yourself and live well.*

21 April 1554

Lionardo

I understand from your letter that Cassandra has been delivered of a beautiful son and that he's fine and that you'll call him Buonarroto; all of which gives me enormous pleasure. Thank God. . . . Thank Cassandra from me and give her my fondest regards. Nothing's new with me. My letter is brief because I'm rushed.

Michelangniolo in Rome

12 January 1562

Lionardo

I received twelve little cheeses some days ago and not only were they delicious, but good to look at. I thank you for them. I didn't write earlier because old age makes writing very difficult. There is nothing new. Now is not the time to visit because I'm in a situation where this would only add to my problems. When it's a good time I'll let you know. . . .

Michelangniolo in Rome

To Giorgio Vasari,
his biographer

Wednesday, 19 September 1554

My dear friend Giorgio,

You'll no doubt say that I'm too old and too crazy to write sonnets, but since people say that I'm in my second childhood already, then I might as well act it out. I see from your letter how much you love me and I'd be very happy to lay these feeble bones next to my father's, as you entreat me. But if I left here now, the whole works programme of St Peter's would be ruined, and it would be a great scandal and a great shame. But when the framework is settled so it cannot be changed, I hope to do as you ask of me, if it's not too sinful to keep that little group of greedy people unhappy a bit longer, who are waiting for me to leave as soon as possible.

Michelangelo Buonarroti in Rome

It is not entirely clear what Michelangelo meant by this last sentence, but he writes elsewhere that he was afraid of the project being altered if he left Rome. He had taken over the position of architect of St Peter's in 1547 for no pay and had battled with Bramante and Sangallo, who had worked on the project before him. The ending of the letter is probably a joke.

Sixteenth-Century Faces

The range of faces shown are all taken from the Sistine Chapel ceiling.

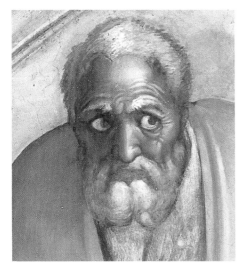

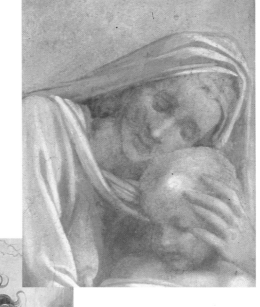

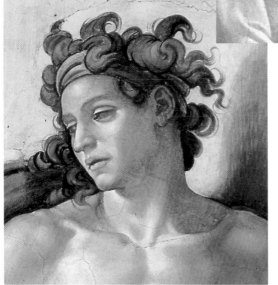

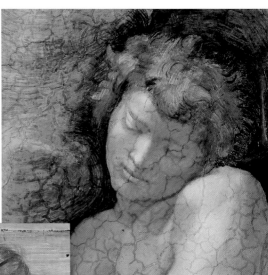

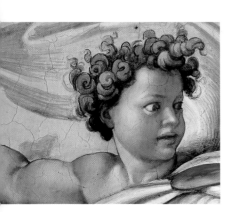

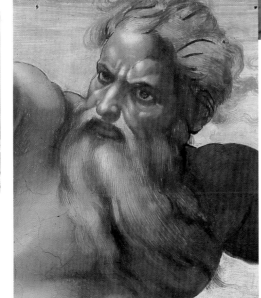

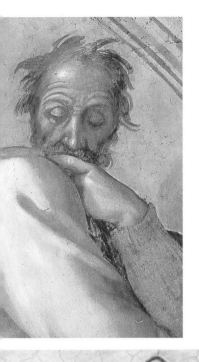
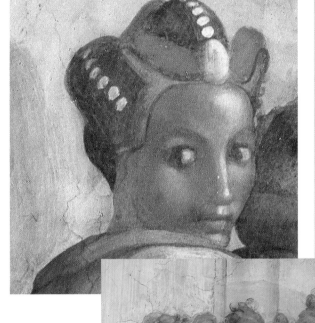
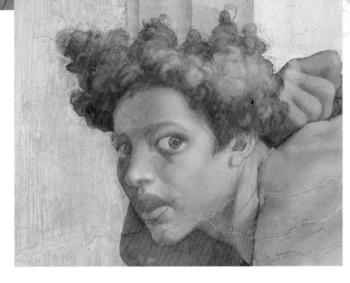
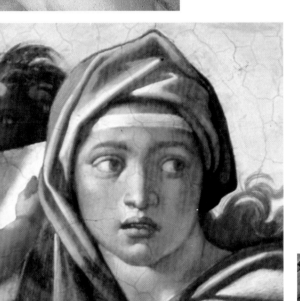
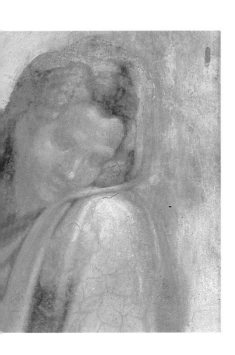
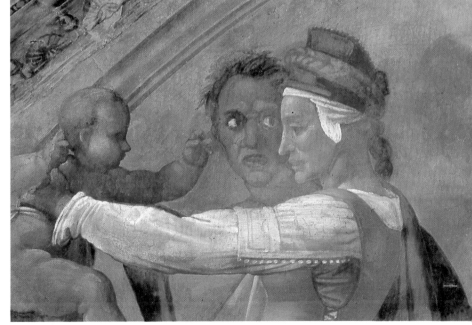

Biographical Sketches

Extracts from the Life of Michelangelo by his friend Ascanio Condivi, 1553

After he finished this work (which was the Battle of the Centaurs), *Lorenzo the Magnificent passed away from this life. Michelangelo returned home to his father and was so grief-stricken by his death that he could do nothing for many days. Then he went and bought a huge piece of marble. . . .*

Michelangelo came to Rome where Pope Julius, still undecided about the tomb, had the idea placed in his head by Bramante and other rivals of Michelangelo, that Michelangelo should paint the vault of Pope Sixtus, inside the Palace, making him believe that Michelangelo would perform miracles. They only did this out of malice, to take the Pope's mind off sculpture, and because they were sure that Michelangelo would not accept the job. This would turn the Pope against him, or if he did accept, he would do the job far less well than Raphael of Urbino, who received favours from those who hated Michelangelo, thinking that Michelangelo's principal art was sculpture (as it really was). Michelangelo who had not worked with colour up to that point, knew that painting a vault was difficult and tried to get out of it, proposing Raphael for the job, making the excuse that it was not his art and he would never succeed. He went on so much about it that the Pope almost exploded with anger. But then seeing his stubbornness, Michelangelo started on the very work that the world sees now with amazement and admiration and which brought him such a reputation that he is above envy. I heard Michelangelo say that it (the chapel) *was not finished as he would have liked because he was impeded by the Pope's haste, who asked him one day when he would finish the chapel and he answered, 'When I can' and he* (the Pope) *said angrily, 'You really want me to have you thrown off the scaffold, don't you?' When Michelangelo heard this, he said to himself, 'No, you will not' and he had the scaffold taken apart, and revealed the work on All Saints Day. It was viewed with great satisfaction by the Pope, who was in the chapel that day, and admired by all Rome. All that needed doing was a retouching with ultramarine and with gold in some places so it would look richer. Julius, whose anger had subsided, wanted this job done by Michelangelo, but Michelangelo,*

Note:
This last sentence is significant in the context of the current restoration which has concluded, correctly in my view, that Michelangelo hardly used the *a secco* technique.

thinking about all the fuss it would cause to put the scaffolding back together again, answered that what was missing was not important. The Pope answered: 'It will still be necessary to retouch it with gold,' and Michelangelo, taking a familiar tone with the Pope as he usually did, said: 'I don't see why men should wear gold' and the Pope replied, 'It will look poor' and Michelangelo replied, 'Those who I have painted here were themselves poor.' So it was made into a joke and things stayed as they were ('e così rimasta').

Michelangelo had 3,000 ducats for his work and expenses, of which I heard he had to spend twenty or twenty-five on colours.

After finishing this work, because of having painted for so long with his eyes raised towards the vault, he could see very little looking downwards, so that if he had to read a letter or look at very small things, he had to hold them over his head with his arms. . . .

Many other things happened to him during the life of Pope Julius, who loved him very much, and was more caring and protective of him than anyone else around him.

That he conceived no ugly thoughts can be seen from the fact that he did not only love human beauty, but all beautiful things universally; a beautiful horse, a beautiful dog, a beautiful country, a beautiful plant, a beautiful mountain, a beautiful wood, and everything beautiful and rare of its kind, admiring them with marvellous affection and so choosing what is beautiful in nature, the way bees gather honey from flowers, using it in their work. . . .

He was always very frugal in his lifestyle, eating more out of necessity than enjoyment, especially when working, and at these times he has been happy with a piece of bread, eating it while working . . . and just as he has eaten little food, so he has slept little. According to him sleep gives him a headache and too much sleep gives him indigestion. When he was stronger, he often slept with all his clothes on and his breeches on his legs, which he wears for cramp which has always bothered him. Sometimes he has left his breeches on so long that when he has removed them, the skin has come off too, like a snake.

Extracts from the Lives of the Artists by Giorgio Vasari, 1568

In the meantime, the Pope had returned to Rome, and Michelangelo was in Bologna finishing the statue (a bronze statue of Pope Julius that was destroyed by the warring Bentivogli and later made into a cannon by the Duke of Ferrara and called irreverently the 'Julia'). *In the absence of Michelangelo, Bramante was plotting with Raphael of Urbino to take the Pope's mind off Michelangelo's finishing the tomb. Bramante was a friend and relation of Raphael of Urbino, and in this respect no friend of Michelangelo, and seeing the Pope's preference for sculpture, managed to get the Pope's attention, and told him that it would be a bad omen to carry on the tomb as it might hurry on the Pope's death, it being a bad idea to create a tomb while he was still alive. They eventually persuaded the Pope to get Michelangelo, on his return, to paint the vault of the chapel created in honour of his uncle Sixtus IV. In this way, Bramante and Michelangelo's other rivals thought that they would get Michelangelo off sculpture in which he reached perfection. They thought that this would make Michelangelo desperate, as he had no experience of working in fresco colours and that he would probably produce very inferior work. . . .*

Some of his Florentine painter friends came down to Rome, to give him help and demonstrate their technique. Among them were Granaccio, Guilian Bugiardini, Iacopo di Sandro, the older Indaco, Agnolo di Donnino, and Aristotile. They were asked to produce some examples, but when he saw their efforts were far away from his expectations, he became fed up and one morning he threw everything they had done away and locked himself up in the chapel and refused to let them in there or in his home. And so this joke seemed to go too far for them and they returned to Florence, ashamed. So Michelangelo decided then to proceed entirely alone on his work, and carried on like this all the way through, working with care, rigour and determination. He saw nobody in case he would have to show his work publicly and thus the most vivid curiosity grew in the public.

Roman lime, being white in colour and made of travertine, does not dry quickly enough and when it is mixed with 'pozzolana' (volcanic dust from Pozzuoli) which is a tawny colour, goes dark and liquid before it dries, and if the wall is very wet, it gets mouldy as it dries. So, this efflorescence appeared in many places, although it disappeared in time with air. When Michelangelo saw what was happening, he despaired of the whole business and did not want to go on. However, His Holiness sent him Giuliano da Sangallo who explained the problem and comforted him and showed him how to remove the mould. Then, when the job was half finished, the Pope who had seen it many times (helped up the ladders by Michelangelo), wanted the public to see it. . . .

Raphael of Urbino, who was an excellent imitator, changed his style upon seeing it, and painted his own interpretation of the Prophets and Sibyls in Santa Maria della Pace to demonstrate his skill, and Bramante tried to get the Pope to give the second half of the ceiling to Raphael . . . but the Pope, growing daily more aware of Michelangelo's skills, and after seeing the first half, wanted Michelangelo to continue with the work, believing that the second half would be even better. So Michelangelo finished the work in twenty months without any help even of a person to grind the colours.

Chronology

1475	Michelangelo Buonarroti born 6 March at Caprese in Tuscany
1477	Construction of Sistine Chapel under Pope Sixtus IV
1481	Michelangelo's mother dies Contract for ten frescoes awarded to Rosselli, Botticelli, Ghirlandaio and Perugino, for side walls of Sistine Chapel
1482	Ghirlandaio replaced by Signorelli
1485	Michelangelo's father remarries. Michelangelo and family move to Via dei Bentacordi, Florence
1488	Apprenticed to the Brothers Ghirlandaio, friendship with Francesco Granacci
1490	Leaves Ghirlandaio workshop for household of Lorenzo de' Medici
1491	*Madonna of the Stairs* (Casa Buonarroti, Florence)
1492	*Battle of the Centaurs* (Casa Buonarroti, Florence) Crucifix for Santo Spirito Church (Casa Buonarroti, Florence) Savonarola rules Florence spiritually with hell-fire sermons Lorenzo dies Piero della Francesca dies
1494	Michelangelo leaves Florence Domenico Ghirlandaio dies Pico della Mirandola, Poliziano, die (philosophers of Medici circle and mentors to Michelangelo)
1494-95	Venice, then to Bologna *Angel and Candelabrum* (S. Domenico Maggiore, Bologna) *St Petronius* (S. Domenico Maggiore, Bologna) *St Proculus* (S. Domenico Maggiore, Bologna)
1495-96	Florence *Cupid* (lost) *St John the Baptist* (lost) Plague in Florence Leonardo da Vinci begins the *Last Supper* in Milan
1497-98	Rome: *Bacchus* (Bargello, Florence)
1497-99	*Pietà* (St Peter's, Rome)
1498	Savonarola burnt at the stake
1499-1502	Raphael studying with Perugino in Perugia
1500	*Entombment* (National Gallery, London, unfinished)
1501	Florence
1501-1504	*David* (Accademia, Florence)
1502	Starts bronze statue of *David* (now lost)
1503	Giuliano della Rovere elected Pope Julius II

1503-1505 *Madonna* (Notre Dame, Bruges)
           Pitti Tondo (Bargello, Florence)

1503-1506 *St Matthew* (unfinished, Accademia, Florence)

1504   *Doni Tondo* (Uffizi, Florence)
           Taddei Tondo (Royal Academy, London)
           Cartoon for uncompleted *Battle of Cascina* (destroyed)

1504-1508 *St Matthew* (Accademia, Florence)

1505   Rome
           First contract for Julius's tomb (the contract is now lost)
           Leaves for the stone quarries of Carrara to choose marble
           for Julius's tomb - away 8 months

1506   *Laocoön* by Agesandros, Polydoros and Athenodoros of
           Rhodes, 1st century BC, dug up in Rome on 14 January,
           in Michelangelo's presence (Vatican, Rome)
           Back to Florence to work on *Battle of Cascina* cartoon
           Dismissed from tomb project in April. Returns to Florence
           First mention of the commission (in a letter) and of Pope
           Julius II's intention to employ Michelangelo on the
           Sistine Chapel

1508   Michelangelo in Florence, in March, where he has been
           engaged on a bronze statue of Julius (erected in
           February 1508, destroyed 30 December 1511)
           Michelangelo signs contract, 10 May, and receives first
           payment for Sistine Chapel ceiling
           Preparatory drawings begun
           Paint ordered from Florence
           Five assistants (*garzoni*) hired and fired
           Scaffolding erected
           Late summer – autumn: Michelangelo begins the painting
           of the eastern half of the chapel
           Raphael working on the *Stanze* in Vatican

1509   January: Work not progressing well. Mould appearing on
           the panel depicting the *Drunkenness of Noah*
           June: Michelangelo becomes ill

1510   July-August: eastern half probably finished around this time
           Sandro Botticelli dies
           Pope in Bologna
           September: Michelangelo keen to resume work, but
           hámpered again by money problems. Leaves Rome for
           Florence to see his father, then to Bologna to see the Pope
           December: from Rome to Bologna again to get money
           from the Pope

1511   January-February: The scaffolding is moved into its new
           position and Michelangelo begins work on the second half.
           Julius is away for months on a military campaign

February: lack of money stops work again
June: Julius returns and Michelangelo is back at work
15 August, Assumption Day: first half of vault unveiled during Vespers and High Mass to the Virgin Mary

1512	Ceiling is finished and is unveiled on the vigil of All Saints Day, 31 October
1513	20 February: Pope Julius II dies, leaving 10,000 ducats to continue the tomb Leo X becomes Pope May: second contract for Julius's tomb Raphael paints last *Stanze* frescoes Machiavelli writes *The Prince*
1513-16	*Bound Slaves* (Louvre, Paris) *Moses* (San Pietro in Vincoli, Rome)
1514	Bramante dies
1515	Pope Leo X commissions Raphael to design tapestries for lower level of Sistine Chapel Michelangelo named Superintendent of Ancient Monuments Ariosto publishes *Orlando Furioso* Thomas More publishes *Utopia*
1516	Third contract for Julius's tomb
1517	Michelangelo in Florence, and at the Carrara and Pietrasanta quarries Martin Luther nails his theses on the door in Wittenberg, marking start of Protestant Reformation Work on Julius's tomb continues Façade for Church of San Lorenzo, Florence
1519-20	*Risen Christ* (Santa Maria Sopra Minerva, Rome)
1519	Leonardo da Vinci dies, aged 67
1519	Raphael's tapestries hung, 19 December
1520-34	Work begun on Medici Chapel in Florence
1520	6 April: Raphael dies, aged 37 Luther declared a heretic
1521-24	Medici Chapel: work continues
1522	25 December: lintel collapses at Sistine Chapel entrance, killing two of the papal Swiss Guards
1523	The Medici Pope, Clement VII, elected
1524	Biblioteca Laurenziana begun. Work on *Dawn* and *Dusk* (Medici Chapels, Florence)
1526	*Night* and *Day* (Medici Chapels, Florence)

1527	Sack of Rome by Charles V's imperial troops Pope imprisoned in Castel Sant' Angelo Medici driven out of Florence
1528	Machiavelli dies Medici Chapel work suspended Michelangelo's brother Buonarroto dies, probably of plague
1529	6 April: Michelangelo employed as military engineer to design fortifications against the Medici, as 'Governatore e Procuratore Generale' September: Michelangelo declared traitor when Florence finally capitulates to Medici
1530	Michelangelo pardoned by Clement VII after two months hiding in a cell underneath the Medici Chapel, on condition that the artist will continue work on the Sistine Chapel *Leda and the Swan*, painting for Duke of Ferrara (destroyed) *Apollo* (Bargello, Florence)
1532	Michelangelo in Rome Fourth contract for Julius's tomb Beginning of deep friendship with Tommaso de' Cavalieri Sells studio in Via Mozza in Florence
1533-34	Receives commission for the *Last Judgement*
1534	Lodovico, his father, dies aged 90 Michelangelo moves permanently to Rome in September Pope Clement VII dies 25 September, and is succeeded by Pope Paul III (Alessandro Farnese) Henry VIII of England declares Church to be part of the 'body politic' and splits from Roman Church Preparatory work begins for the *Last Judgement* Martin Luther's translation of the Bible into German
1535	Pope Paul III, following Pope Clement's wishes, orders scaffolding to be built for the painting of the *Last Judgement* Michelangelo named 'Supreme Architect, Sculptor and Painter' of the papal palace by Pope Paul III
1536	Meets Vittoria Colonna, Marchioness of Pescara Michelangelo starts painting the *Last Judgement* on the altar wall, destroying two of his earlier lunettes of the Sistine ceiling cycle, and blocking up two windows
1538	Antique equestrian statue of Marcus Aurelius erected in the Campidoglio, Rome, with pedestal designed by Michelangelo
1539-40	*Brutus* (Bargello, Florence)
1541	31 October: the *Last Judgement* unveiled (exactly 29 years to the day after the ceiling)

1542-45	*Leah* and *Rachel* created for Julius's tomb Fifth contract for the tomb
1542-50	Pauline Chapel begun: *1. Conversion of Paul, 2. Crucifixion of Peter* (Pope's private chapel in the Vatican)
1543	The astronomer Copernicus publishes his astronomical system, in which the Earth is no longer assumed to be at the centre of the Universe
1544	June: Michelangelo ill
1545	Counter-Reformation begins to combat rapidly spreading Protestant movement Statues designed for Julius's tomb (*Moses, Rachel, Leah*) finally installed in San Pietro in Vincoli, Rome (unused *Slaves* scattered, some to the Strozzi family, and then to France, some to Cosimo I for the Boboli Gardens, Florence)
1546-50	Michelangelo takes over construction drawings of the Palazzo Farnese from Antonio da Sangallo Redesigns the Campidoglio (Rome's civic capitol) Wins competition to redesign façade of Palazzo Farnese, Rome, after original architect Antonio da Sangallo dies in 1546
1547	Vittoria Colonna dies Sebastiano del Piombo, follower of Michelangelo, dies Official appointment by Pope Paul III as architect of St Peter's, on no pay Paolo Giovio mentions to Vasari that the Sistine Chapel ceiling appears to be in a 'poor condition' Begins *Deposition of Christ* (Museo del Opera del Duomo, Florence)
1549	Marcello Venusti, follower of Michelangelo, copies *Last Judgement* in miniature, showing 'indecent' nudity of original (see also entry for 1564)
1550	Architectural designs for façade of Palazzo Farnese, Rome First edition of Vasari's *Lives* published
1553	Condivi's *Life of Michelangelo* published Floor of Biblioteca Laurenziana designed
1555	Death of Michelangelo's assistant, Francesco Amadori (l'Urbino), after twenty-six years of service and friendship Michelangelo's brother Sigismondo dies *Palestrina Pietà* (Accademia, Florence)
1555-56	*Rondanini Pietà* begun (Castello Sforzesco, Milan) September-October: in Spoleto
1558	Designs stairs for Biblioteca Laurenziana, finished later by Ammanati from Michelangelo's model Starts designs for model of dome for St Peter's (finished 1561, built after Michelangelo's death by Giacomo della Porta and others)
1561	Architectural work on ancient Roman gate, the Porta Pia
1561	Finishes wooden model of dome of St Peter's

1564	Michelangelo dies 18 February in Rome, at the age of nearly 90, with Tommaso de' Cavalieri, his servant Antonio, Daniele da Volterra and two doctors at his bedside Soon after Michelangelo's death, Da Volterra (Daniele Ricciarelli) is employed to paint breeches and loin cloths over the naked figures of the *Last Judgement*, thereby assuming the nickname *Il braghettone*, 'the breech maker' 10 March: Michelangelo's coffin arrives secretly in Florence 12 March: coffin taken to Santa Croce, where it now lies April: William Shakespeare born 14 July: Michelangelo's memorial service held in Medici church of San Lorenzo. Benedetto Varchi gives two-hour oration
1566	Domenico Carnevali retouches *Noah's Sacrifice*, probably repainting female figure in left foreground. Matteo da Lecce and Hendrick van der Broeck repaint damaged frescoes on entrance wall
1568	Second edition of Vasari's *Life of Michelangelo*
1572	Carnevali applies wax and resin to ceiling cracks
1625	Pope Urban VIII commissions Lagi to clean the ceiling of the Sistine Chapel
1710-12	Pope Clement XI commissions Mazzuoli's restoration Glue probably applied to ceiling
1762	Pozzi's restoration and more covering-up of nudes in the *Last Judgement*
1797	Explosion in nearby Castel Sant' Angelo causes part of the *Flood* to crash to the floor and also an *ignudo* (left of the Delphic Sibyl) to be destroyed
1825	Camuccini cleans some of the ceiling and the *Last Judgement*
1885	Michelangelo's studio and home at Macel de' Corvi ('the crow market') destroyed to make the 'wedding cake', the Victor Emmanuel monument in Rome
1904-1905	Restoration of Sistine Chapel ceiling and of the *Last Judgement* by Cingolani and Cecconi-Principi
1936-38	Restoration work carried out by Biagetti
1961-74	Restoration by Redig de Campos of fifteenth-century wall frescoes
1980-89	Cleaning of Michelangelo's lunettes and later of the vault begins under GianLuigi Colalucci
1989	31 October: cleaning of the Sistine Chapel ceiling finished (477 years exactly to the day since Michelangelo completed it)
1990	March: scaffolding erected for restoration work on the *Last Judgement*. Researches begin

Glossary

A.B.57 The cleaning agent used in the current restoration of the Sistine Chapel. Used in cleaning fresco for the last fifteen years, it appears to have no side effects. It is composed of a dilute mixture of ammonium bicarbonate, sodium bicarbonate, desogen and carboxymethycellulose in distilled water. It is left on the fresco for a maximum of three minutes.

Arriccio The penultimate layer of rough plaster under the final *intonaco*.

A secco The technique in which paint is applied to already completed fresco work. The subject of some controversy in the restoration work being carried out on the Sistine Chapel ceiling.

Bramante (1444?-1514) Great architect of the High Renaissance and rival of Michelangelo. Trained by Piero della Francesca and Mantegna.

Contrapposto Literally, 'counterpoised' in Italian, referring to the position of many of Michelangelo's nudes, both painted and sculpted, which are weighted in two directions. The hips might be facing one way, and the shoulders in another direction, causing a twist in the axis of the spine. This is also called 'torsion'.

Cartoon A large drawing on paper which is used to transfer an image to the wall for fresco. The lines of the drawing are pricked with small holes, the cartoon is temporarily glued to the wall, and fine charcoal dust is blown through the holes. The image appears as a series of small dots. Alternatively the lines are actually drawn through the paper with a sharp point.

Fresco The technique (see Chapter 5) in which water-based paint is applied to damp plaster, forming a chemical bond which renders the painting permanent and waterproof.

Genii The children that accompany the Prophets and Sibyls and appear to embody their thoughts.

Gilding The use of gold leaf on the medallions held by the *ignudi*.

Giotto (1266/67-1337) Florentine painter of the Early Renaissance.

Ignudi The muscular seated male figures on the Sistine Chapel ceiling, who hold the medallions with ribbons and oak leaves.

Intonaco The final layer of plaster, to which the paint is applied.

Leonardo da Vinci (1452-1519) One of the greatest thinkers of the Renaissance, a consummate artist but also a scientist, inventor, architect and philosopher.

Lunettes Semi-circular panels over the Sistine Chapel windows depicting the ancestors of Christ.

Masaccio Tommaso di Ser Giovanni di Mone, born 1401, died *circa* 1428, great master of fifteenth-century painting, and powerful influence on Michelangelo. Nicknamed Masaccio, or Big Tom.

Medallions Gilded circular discs depicting on the Sistine Chapel ceiling biblical struggles from the Book of Kings.

Paraloid B 72 The acrylic resin

used by the restorers to protect the water-soluble '*a secco*' areas from being washed away by the A.B.57 medium.

Pendentives The sections of painting between the lunettes that hold the *putti* (cherubs), bearing name plates of the Prophets and Sibyls.

Perspective A mathematical system, devised by Brunelleschi and Piero della Francesca in the early fifteenth century, used by painters to achieve three-dimensional effects in a two-dimensional medium. The premise behind this system of perspective is that parallel lines appear to meet though they never do so in reality. The road is bordered by parallel lines which never really come together, but appear to meet on the horizon.

Perugino (c.1445-1523) Painter. Possibly a pupil of Piero della Francesca. Teacher of Raphael. Painted in the Sistine Chapel.

Piero della Francesca (1410/20-1492) One of the most important painters of the fifteenth century.

Pigment Another word for paint, though referring usually to its raw state, in mineral or earth form.

Pope List of Popes during Michelangelo's lifetime:
Sixtus IV (della Rovere family) 1471-84
Innocent VIII (Cibo) 1484-92
Alexander VI (Borgia) 1492-1503
Pius III (Todeschini-Piccolomini) 1503 (10 days!)
Julius II (della Rovere) 1503-1513
Leo X (Medici) 1513-1521
Adrian VI (Florenz, from Utrecht) 1522-23
Clement VII (Medici) 1523-34
Paul III (Farnese) 1534-49
Julius III (del Monte) 1550-55
Marcellus II (Cervini) 1555 (3 weeks)
Paul IV (Carafa) 1555-59
Pius IV (Medici) 1559-65

Putti Cherubs, childlike angelic figures that support the cornices holding the *ignudi*.

Quarry Place of excavation of stone used for building or sculpture, in Michelangelo's case, usually Carrara.

Raphael (1483-1520) Raffaello Sanzio, youngest of three great masters of the Italian Renaissance. In Rome from 1508, contemporary and rival of Michelangelo.

Spandrels The four large triangular corner panels depicting
David and Goliath
Judith and Holofernes
The Brazen Serpent
The Punishment of Haman
and the smaller panels depicting the ancestors of Christ.

Terribiltà Literally 'terribleness', an expression used by Michelangelo's biographers to denote his 'terrible', awe-inspiring genius.

Vault The shape of the roof of the Sistine Chapel, like the rounded shape of a barrel halved lengthways.

Selected Bibliography

Barocchi, P. *Giorgio Vasari; La Vita di Michelangelo nelle redazioni del 1550 e del 1568*, Milan and Naples, 1962

Barocchi, P., & Ristori (Eds.) *Il Carteggio di Michelangelo*, Florence, 1965–68

Blunt, A. *Artistic Theory in Renaissance Italy 1450–1600*, Oxford University Press, 1961

Buonarroti, M. *Le Rime* (Barelli, E., Ed.) Rizzoli, Milan, 1987

Condivi, A. (Transl. by Wohl, A. & H.) *Life of Michelangelo*, Oxford, 1976

Condivi, A. *Vita de Michelangelo Buonarroti*, (Barelli, E., Ed.) Milan, 1964

De Tolnay, C. *Michelangelo (5 vols.)*, Princeton, 1943–1960

De Vecchi, P.L. *Studi sulla poesia di Michelangelo, Giornale Storico della Letteratura Italiana*, 1963

Freedberg, S.J. *Painting of the High Renaissance in Rome and Florence (2 vols.)* Harvard University Press, Cambridge MA, 1961

Giacometti, M. (Ed.) *Michelangelo Rediscovered*, Muller, Blond & White, London, 1986

Gilbert, C. *Complete poems and selected letters of Michelangelo*, New York, 1963

Girardi, E.N. *Rime di Michelangelo Buonarroti*, Bari, 1960

Hare, C. *Most Illustrious Ladies of the Italian Renaissance*, London, 1904

Hartt, F. *A History of Italian Renaissance Art, 2nd ed.*, Thames and Hudson, London, 1987

Hartt, F., Mancinelli, F., & Colalucci, G. (Okamura, T., Photographer) *The Sistine Chapel (2 vols.)*, Barrie & Jenkins, London, and Alfred A. Knopf, New York, 1991

Hibbard, H. *Michelangelo*, Pelican, London *(2 vols.)*, 1985

Jeffery, D. 'A Renaissance for Michelangelo,' *National Geographic* (176, No. 6) 1989

Jennings, E. (Trans.) *The Sonnets of Michelangelo*, London, 1961

Mancinelli, F., Colalucci, G., & Gabrielli, N. *The Restoration of the Sistine Chapel, Scienza e Tecnica*, Edizioni Mondadori, Milan, 1987–88

Milanesi, H. *Le Lettere di Michelangelo Buonarroti edite ed inedite coi ricordi ed i contrati*, Florence, 1875

Murray, L. *Michelangelo*, Thames and Hudson, London, 1980

Papafava, F. (Ed.) *The Sistine Chapel*, Vatican, 1986

Ramsden, E.H. (Ed. and Trans.) *Letters of Michelangelo*, Peter Owen, 1963

Rollond, R. *Michelangelo*, Heinemann, 1912

Seymour, C. (Ed.) *The Sistine Chapel Ceiling*, W.W. Norton, New York, and Thames and Hudson, London, 1972

Stokes, A. *Critical Writings Vol III*, Thames and Hudson, London, 1978

Symonds, J.A. *Sonnets of Michelangelo*, London 1897

Vasari, G. (Trans. by Bull, G.) *Life of Michelangelo Buonarroti,* London, 1971

Wadley, N. *Michelangelo*, Spring Books, London, 1965

Weil-Garris Brandt, K. 'Twenty-five questions about Michelangelo's Sistine Ceiling,' *Apollo (CXXVI* No. 310) 1987

Wilde, J. 'The Decoration of the Sistine Chapel,' *Proceedings of the British Academy XLIV* 1958